BULBS
THE FOUR SEASONS

BULBS

THE FOUR SEASONS

A GUIDE TO SELECTING AND GROWING BULBS ALL YEAR ROUND

BRIAN MATHEW

PAVILION

It gives me great pleasure to dedicate this book to our old friend Wayne Roderick. His inimitable hospitality and great generosity in sharing his wide knowledge of Californian bulbs with us and with many others over the years is much appreciated.

First published in Great Britain in 1998 by
Pavilion Books Limited
London House
Great Eastern Wharf
Parkgate Road
London SW11 4NQ

Designed by Andrew Barron & Collis Clements Associates

A CIP catalogue record for this book is available from the British Library

ISBN 1-85793-504-7

Typeset in Garamond
Printed and bound in Singapore by Kyodo

10 9 8 7 6 5 4 3 2 1

This book may be ordered by post direct from the publisher. Please contact the Marketing Department. But try your bookshop first.

Half-title page: Bulbs often look most effective when combined with other plants. Here *Muscari latifolium* grows through *Euphorbia myrsinites*.

Title page: The famous laburnum arch at Barnsley House, Gloucestershire, England contains an interesting blend of rounded hebes and *Allium* heads contrasting with spiky *Eremurus*.

CONTENTS

FOREWORD

As my mentor in the 1960s, the great English bulb grower Bertram Anderson, once said: 'Effort is the sauce of life and success its reward'. There can be few more satisfying achievements than to plant dry bulbs, cosset them for a while and then see them burst into life a few months later. Bulbous plants form the mainstay of our spring and autumn gardens, for they are designed to exploit the early and late seasons when few other plants are in flower. Some bulbs can burst into growth immediately the winter shows the slightest sign of abating or, in the case of autumn-flowering species, as soon as there is a hint of rain. Others, for example the stately lilies, take a little longer to develop and provide us with a summer display while just a valuable few bloom in the depths of winter.

With a charming structural simplicity, bulbous plants can be used to great advantage in the garden to contrast or harmonize with perennials and shrubs. This book describes the attributes, of a a wide range of bulbs for every season, and how they might be featured in association with other subjects in the garden.

Ever-popular snowdrops form a perfectly natural association with winter aconites.

INTRODUCTION

I t is probably true to say that bulbs are more popular today than they have ever been, certainly in terms of the numbers sold and the range available, but interest in them can be traced back for thousands of years.

Early records are few, but we can glean some details from the ancient writers, such as Theophrastus and Dioscorides, and it is clear that the Greeks were greatly interested in some of their native bulbous plants. Undoubtedly they appreciated the beauty of the wild flowers, but their interest in them focused mainly on their usefulness. A classical example is the saffron crocus, an autumn-flowering species producing a red, curiously fragrant spice which has been, and still is, one of the most sought-after and expensive in the world, used as a dye, as a flavouring and colouring agent in cooking, and for a wide range of medicinal purposes. It was known to the Minoans on Crete and to the early inhabitants of the Aegean island of Thera, where frescoes have been found depicting lady saffron-gatherers; so its history goes back at least 3,500 years.

There are plenty of other examples. Garlic, a member of the onion family, is known to have been used by the ancient Egyptians, and leeks also appear to have been popular at a very early time. The tassel hyacinth was made into an unpleasant-sounding cream by the Greeks, Dioscorides noting that it would 'taketh away the piles, being roasted and mixed with burnt heads of fishes'; while the bulbs, used as a poultice, were 'good for laxations, bruises, splinters and for the griefs of the joints and for gangrenes and gouts'.

Interest in bulbs for medicinal purposes continued unabated through the ages and, in Europe, the Middle Ages were a golden time for the herbalist-physicians. Many of the volumes published at this time were still based on the work of the Greeks, with modifications and additions as new plants were discovered and introduced into cultivation. In the late sixteenth century, the oft-quoted John Gerard brought together much previously published work in his *Herball or Generall Historie of Plantes*, in which we can find descriptions of plants including many bulbs. Gerard was still publicizing bulbs primarily for their useful characteristics, although it is clear that by this time they were also becoming appreciated more for aesthetic purposes as garden plants. So we find that familiar plants such as the dog's tooth violet (*Erythronium dens-canis*), which today is grown purely for ornamental reasons, was, in Gerard's time, used for a variety of purposes; it was, for example, 'put in children's pottage against worms of the belly' and was recommended (as were many other plants) as an aphrodisiac, the

optimistic claim being that 'it provoketh bodily lust if it be only handled but much more if it be drunk with wine'.

The sixteenth century saw a great upsurge of interest in bulbs as garden plants, notably those from Asia Minor, where the Ottoman Turks were developing the native species in a very sophisticated manner. The remarkable story of the introduction of tulips to Europe from Istanbul (Constantinople) in the mid sixteenth century by Busbecq, the Austrian Ambassador to Suleiman the Magnificent, has been told many times, but it serves to identify the beginning of a fascination with bulbs that led to the formation of the great Dutch bulb industry and rapidly spread throughout Europe, continuing unabated to the present day. When Busbecq visited Istanbul, the Turks were cultivating an abundance of flowers, including tulips, hyacinths and crown imperials. Although at first they would have grown the wild forms, these were developed so that at the height of the tulip's popularity there were some 1,500 varieties, which were given awards and cultivar names by 'flower councils' and were recorded by artists. The colour illustrations of tulips and hyacinths are still in existence in the Topkapi library in Istanbul, bearing witness to the skill of these early plant breeders.

In Europe, the main interest in bulbs has always centred on those from the Mediterranean region, the Near and Middle East and central Asia, since not only are there many colourful subjects throughout this area, but they are also hardy in much of the European continent. Bulbs from other areas have had their periods of

popularity. As North America was opened up and botanists began to explore this vast area, many interesting bulbs came to light. The huge range of amazing bulbs from the floristically rich south-west Cape region of South Africa caused a great stir when they were first discovered and introduced to the gardens of Europe, but these – and even more so those from the tropics – required glasshouses, so they were left largely in the care of botanic gardens and the wealthier private gardeners of the early nineteenth century, who could afford the running costs and a team of gardeners to provide detailed attention. Later, exploration in China resulted in spectacular introductions, particularly of shrubs, but there were also some notable bulb discoveries, such as the beautiful *Lilium regale*, introduced by Ernest Wilson in 1903.

The two world wars probably resulted in the loss of many of the more unusual and 'difficult' plants that had been introduced (in addition to many of the people who were skilled in growing them), but today interest in bulbs has reached an unprecedented level of popularity. Horticulture in the second half of this century has seen a tremendous boom, particularly with regard to 'enthusiast gardening'. Now it is possible to find highly specialized groups, sometimes devoted individuals, focusing their attention on a narrow range of plants, or even a single genus. There has also been a great upsurge of interest in the wild species, as opposed to their large and gaudy hybrid derivatives, no doubt greatly encouraged by today's ease of travel. Anywhere in the world can now be reached within a matter of hours, so

**A striking display
of flamboyant
parrot tulips and
forget-me-nots.**

previously little-known plants, sometimes new to science, can be growing a few days later thousands of miles away in a specialist's garden. The matter of conservation has therefore become an emotive subject.

What of the future? Clearly plant breeders will continue their quest for novelties and, with genetic manipulation already well established, this will become ever more sophisticated. Red crocuses and blue lilies will be a formality, provided that the cost of development is deemed worth while. This will be fun and will provide an increasing range of plants for our gardens, but it is perhaps much more important that we do not lose sight of the original wild species. Ideally, we must encourage their conservation in the wild, in the habitats in which they have evolved over millions of years, but we must also strive to perfect our cultivation techniques so that, once introduced, continual replacement from the wild becomes unnecessary.

Note about Name Changes

It undoubtedly irritates some (many!) gardeners that well-known names change from time to time, apparently at the whim of the botanist. This book is no exception, in that some names are used that may be unfamiliar to the reader.

There are three basic reasons for such changes. First, due to misidentification: it may be that, at some time in the past, a plant has been misnamed and has become well known under that name before research shows that it should, in fact, be called something else. Second, there are name changes caused by the application of the International Code of Botanical Nomenclature or its horticultural counterpart, the ICNCP (International Code of Nomenclature of Cultivated Plants); one of the rules is that the earliest name to be published, subsequent to Linnaeus' system of nomenclature (that is, from 1753 onwards), is the correct one. Thus it often happens that a literature search reveals an older name than the one

in current use, resulting in a name change if the rules are to be adhered to. The third reason for name changes is because of botanical research. A botanist may, for instance, decide – in the light of new knowledge – that two plants formerly recognized as two separate species are in fact just variations of one; the name that applies to the combined species has to be the earliest one published and may not necessarily be the one most familiar to gardeners.

Situations can arise where name changes involve more than one of these reasons. To give an example, it was decided for botanical reasons that the well-known Scarborough lily, *Vallota*, was really insufficiently different from *Cyrtanthus* to merit recognition as a separate genus, so its one species, *V. speciosa*, was transferred to *Cyrtanthus*; for nomenclatural reasons (priority), the species name changed to *elatus*, resulting in *Cyrtanthus elatus*.

This is an oversimplification, but it gives some idea as to the reasons behind the apparently whimsical ways of botanists!

A naturalized drift of *Scilla siberica* and *Chionodoxa*, following hard on the heels of snowdrops and winter aconites in early spring.

INTRODUCING
THE WORLD OF BULBS

WHY ARE THERE BULBOUS PLANTS?

Bulbs, and other similar underground swollen storage organs like corms, tubers and rhizomes, represent one of those neat tricks of nature that allow plants to deal with almost any of the many environments on Earth. Some plants drop their leaves during cold winters; some have large fleshy stems covered with spines for protection; some behave as annuals and grow only when there is sufficient warmth and moisture; some trap insects for their food; and others live up in the air on trees, utilizing sunlight and the moisture in the air to manufacture their food. It is all a question of adapting to occupy a niche in the many different situations provided by our amazing world – a niche that may result from a variety of factors, such as climate, geography and geology, and often from a combination of these with others.

The regions of the world with a climate that is warm and dry in summer, and damp and cold in winter, pose a particular problem in that the period when both moisture and warmth are combined is very short. In the Mediterranean and Middle East, for

Right: Tulips in Turkey. Bulbous plants such as this have evolved an underground storage system for survival through the coming dry period.

Opposite top: Many bulbs burst into growth in early spring for a short growing season before the long dry summer. *Crocus gargaricus* **in Turkey.**
Bottom: Autumn bulbs give us a valuable final display before winter sets in. Many of them produce their leaves later on, in spring. *Colchicum speciosum.*

example, a long hot summer of about six months is an adverse time for most plants, as is the winter, so many of the plants fit their growing cycle into the short spring, after the soil has warmed and before the dry summer has set in. Anyone visiting the Mediterranean and similar climatic areas of the world will often find a wonderful display of colourful annuals making use of this seasonal niche, but these have to

develop from seedling stage to flowering in one season, so they do not usually flower until late spring or early summer. Bulbs, however, have perhaps 'gone one better' along this road of niche-finding. They are perennials that have developed a swollen fleshy storage system underground, able to survive long dry periods but equally able to burst into life as soon as favourable weather arrives, so they tend to be the first plants to flower in spring and autumn.

There are bulbs in flower at almost every time of the year, which makes them especially useful as garden plants, so we will start by taking a look at their growth patterns and origins. This will help us understand why they flower at the times they do, and how this affects their cultivation requirements.

THE FOUR SEASONS

Spring bulbs

Most of the spring bulbs do in fact start to make root growth in the autumn (this is why nurseries and garden centres sell bulbs for planting in the early autumn), but they remain below ground throughout the cool winter until the warmth of the spring sunshine triggers aerial growth. Many of them already have flower buds, formed within the bulbs during the previous summer's 'dormant' period (so it is not really a proper dormancy), so that when warmth and moisture combine they are able to flower almost immediately. This is why much of our very early spring colour in the garden is provided by bulbs – crocuses, snowdrops, daffodils, scillas, hyacinths, and so on – long before the annuals and many of the non-bulbous perennials have begun to grow. Having flowered, these spring bulbs ripen and shed their seeds, then die down below ground to their storage organs to sit out the adverse period of drought ahead. Spring, therefore, is the prime time for bulbs, and without them our gardens would be dull for several months before the main flush of perennials, shrubs and annuals. Many of the spring-flowering bulbs are natives of mountainous regions, flowering at the onset of warmer weather, and are to be found in the hills and mountains especially of southern Europe, North Africa, western and central Asia, North and South America and southern Africa.

Autumn bulbs

Autumn too is a good time for bulbs, and a visit to parts of the Mediterranean and western Asia will reveal many bulbs adapted to flower at this time – a sort of second spring. In a way, these autumnal bulbs make even better use of the short growing season. They behave in exactly the same way as the spring-bloomers, in that they form flower buds inside the bulb in summer and start into root growth at the onset of the autumn rains, but in their case they burst into flower immediately in the autumn while the weather, and the soil, is reasonably warm. This has the great advantage that their flowering stage, including pollination and fertilization, is completed in the autumn when there are few other plants with which to compete for insects. Many of them then disappear for the colder winter months, so that there is nothing exposed to the elements. Then, when the short spring arrives, all that remains to be done to complete the annual cycle is to produce leaves and seed pods, all the other stages having been completed. Autumn-flowering bulbs occur especially in the Mediterranean region and western Asia, although there are also some in southern Africa, for example the nerines.

This explains the reason for the many spring and autumn bulbs that are available to enhance our gardens at these potentially dull times, but what of the winter months?

Winter bulbs

Obviously, there are fewer candidates for the winter months, but those that there are, are extremely valuable. Although the result is the same – the provision of flowers in winter – there are two rather different categories of winter bulb.

The first group consists of those that grow at low altitudes in mild conditions in the wild. They naturally flower in the winter, while the weather is cool and moist compared with the summer, but not harshly cold. The Algerian iris,

Iris unguicularis, and some of the dwarf narcissi such as *Narcissus cantabricus* and *N. romieuxii* are good examples, their delicate flowers appearing from late autumn to early spring. Many of the South African bulbs from the south-west Cape (mainly winter rainfall) region also fall into this category. Unfortunately, for those gardening in many parts of Britain, Europe and North America, they are not frost-hardy so must be grown with some form of protection in winter.

The other group of bulbs that can be useful winter-flowering subjects in our gardens are those from colder, higher-altitude areas. They normally flower in spring when the snow melts but, when brought to lower-altitude, milder gardens, often flower earlier on in the winter. Perhaps one of the best examples is *Cyclamen coum* from the western Asiatic mountains, which will often flower in the depths of winter and is very hardy, originating as it does from regions with low winter temperatures.

A lot of those bulbs that naturally flower in early spring around melting snow patches in the mountains can be regarded as suitable for providing winter colour in our gardens, so it is possible to have a good winter display using the earlier species of *Crocus*, *Galanthus* and *Eranthis*. These winter-flowering bulbs are much the same as the autumn and spring ones in their growth patterns, making their root growth in the autumn and dying down for the summer months.

Summer bulbs

Bulbs for flowering in the summer months have been left to last since they are completely different in their behaviour from those of the other three seasons and originate from quite separate climatic areas of the world.

Although our summer gardens are full of colour, provided by a host of perennials, trees, shrubs and annuals, there is a place for the summer bulbs, since their flowers often have a charming simplicity and their upright, frequently spiky stature provides useful contrast. Interestingly, most summer bulbs are fairly tall compared with their autumn/winter/spring relatives, which are primarily dwarf – a difference of form that is no doubt largely due to the better and longer growing conditions of the summer months. They are also fundamentally different in their cultural requirements,

since they have evolved in a quite distinct type of climate. The summer bulbs still have to overcome a dry period – that is, after all, the reason for having a bulb – but in their case the dry period comes in winter and the moister warmer weather in summer; these bulbs lie cool, dry and dormant in winter, then start into growth at the onset of warm spring weather and continue to grow and flower throughout the summer. They can be thought of as 'summer rainfall bulbs' since they originate from those areas of the world receiving mainly summer rainfall. The monsoon areas of eastern Asia are a good source of lilies, for example, while the eastern Cape 'summer rainfall' region of southern Africa provides us with valuable bulbs such as *Gladiolus*, *Galtonia* and *Eucomis*. And the gaudy, dramatic *Tigridia* originates from parts of Mexico that are dry in winter and moist in summer. Not surprisingly, summer bulbs are mostly to be found on sale in spring, for planting as soon as the soil has begun to warm up.

Above: Summer bulbs, such as lilies, are dormant from autumn to spring, the reverse of the 'winter-growing' bulbs. *Lilium henryi.*

Opposite: Winter-flowering bulbs are few, but they have great impact in the garden. *Crocus tommasinianus* **appears as soon as the days begin to lengthen.**

GARDEN HABITATS
FOR BULBS

Perhaps more surprising than what we cannot grow in our gardens is what we *can* grow. The average garden contains plants that have originated from all over the world, all growing relatively happily side by side, providing that the gardener has chosen appropriate individual sites. With bulbous plants it is possible to grow a representative collection from all the continents where bulbs occur, and Antarctica is the only continent where they do not, as far as I know!

Left: In late spring, a spot in the dappled shade provides a perfect home for *Cyclamen repandum* and wood anemones. Right: Snowdrops, Corydalis and dog's tooth violets in a shady part of the author's garden.

Dappled shade provides ideal conditions for this delightful group of mixed bulbs at the National Trust garden of Knightshayes Court in Devonshire, England.

THE NATURAL HABITATS OF BULBS

Before going on to the garden situation, it is worth looking briefly at the various places in which bulbs occur in the wild, inasmuch as it affects our choice of site in the garden. Since bulbs have evolved in order to enable the plant to survive through a dry (often also warm) period, it is not surprising that the vast majority occur in open situations where there is little shade from other vegetation. Some grow among grasses and small herbaceous plants, but very few are found in woods or damp situations, although among these few are some highly attractive garden plants. The hardy bulbs from seasonally dry, temperate

regions with cool winters are by far the most plentiful in the world, and are understandably the most popular with 'temperate' gardeners, but there are bulbs that occur in the tropics, again in those areas where there are marked dry and wet seasons. The cultivation of tropical bulbs differs from that of hardy bulbs, since they react mainly to being wet or dry, with little or no associated temperature change. Bulbs from the south-west Cape region, and many of those from temperate South America, are similar in their cultivation requirements to those from the Mediterranean area, but differ subtly in that most are not quite frost-hardy, so in cold areas they are ideal subjects for a slightly heated conservatory.

We will now look at the various sites for bulbs, starting at the 'shady end' with those that are woodlanders, progressing on to those that grow in meadows, and then to the largest and horticulturally most significant group, occurring in open situations with a little competition and protection from other plants, but not enough to cause significant shade. The extreme of this is the open rocky or sandy site, which becomes totally sun-baked in the summer, and where there is scarcely any protection from other plants; bulbs from such sites often require specialized treatment. We will also take a separate look at Cape bulbs and tropical bulbs.

Some bulbs, such as the snake's head fritillary, are natives of grassy meadows and this effect may be duplicated in the garden.

Bulbs for the shade

Although most bulbs grow in the open, there are some well-known exceptions that occur in dappled shade, such as snowdrop, winter aconite, cyclamen, bluebell, trillium and the dog's tooth violet. Although this may at first appear contradictory – why have a bulb growing in cool shade? – it must be remembered that trees and shrubs use up large quantities of moisture in summer and the soil where the bulbs occur can be quite dry; between autumn and spring the bulbs are in growth but the trees are leafless, allowing rain and sun to penetrate and provide for the needs of the bulbs beneath. In gardens we can make great use of these lovely plants, even if we

have only one or two small deciduous trees or shrubs. Their cultivation is simple, since these bulbs are used to coping with competition and require only an initially well-prepared soil with extra humus, then an annual top-dressing of well-decayed compost or leafmould to simulate the rotting leaves of their natural habitat.

Bulbs in grassland

Quite a number of bulbs occur in meadows in the wild and these too are, on the whole, also easy to cultivate, since they grow naturally in close association with other plants and are not subjected to climatic extremes. Much the same conditions apply to these bulbs as to those in wooded

situations, as grass makes its main growth when the bulbs are dying down for their rest period. There is little shade when the bulbs are in flower, but later on the grass grows up and shades the ground, keeping it relatively cool. Bulbs that grow in grassland – for example, the snake's head fritillary, the summer snowflake, many of the daffodils and some crocuses – are therefore not hot and dry during their dormant period and can be cultivated without special treatment. They can, of course, be planted in grass in the garden, and an area of rough grass can form a very attractive 'natural' feature.

Bulbs for open situations

Most of the bulbs we grow require open situations in well-drained soils that become warm and dry in summer. Open sunny borders are ideal for the taller narcissi and tulips forming the backbone of a mid-spring display, either in mixed informal plantings or in bedding schemes. The smaller species need to be planted at the front of borders or in rock gardens. Although the rock garden is not often seen as a garden feature nowadays, it does provide an ideal habitat for small bulbs, in that the rock pockets drain well and are nearer to eye level, a factor that may be attractive to those of advancing years! Raised beds are an easier way of achieving this and are an excellent home for a wide range of small bulbs, as well as forming an interesting garden feature. The bed can be quite simple, using natural or reconstituted stone for the walls, dry or cemented, and of any shape, depending upon the formality or informality required; the height also depends upon taste and cost. Higher walls, up to about 45 cm (18 in), will allow room for plants in the crevices. After constructing the walls, the existing soil is broken up and sharp sand and gravel incorporated, then the bed is filled to the top with a soil/grit mixture (about 50:50). A topping of grit looks attractive, deters weeds (perhaps also slugs and snails), and prevents the surface from becoming panned during heavy rain. I find that the upkeep of raised beds is minimal. To provide interest when the bulbs are dormant, I grow various compact perennials and shrubs, particularly those with small or grey foliage, such as lavender,

Sunny borders provide suitable situations for a wide variety of bulbs. Tulips are especially effective when used informally in mixed borders.

rosemary, thyme, marjoram and grey helichrysums, and these will tolerate some summer drought. I can thoroughly recommend this type of gardening for anyone who likes small bulbs but has a garden in a rainy climate and heavy or damp soil.

Bulbs from hot, dry places

This is an extreme situation, where bulbs are growing in bare rocky or sandy situations with little protection from other plants, and where they get thoroughly sun-baked during the summer dormant period. Such bulbs often require rather specialized treatment in gardens, in the form of protection under glass – not so much from cold winters but from excess rain in summer while they are at rest and needing to be warm and dry. Good examples of this group are the irises from the Middle East and the *Calochortus* from California, many of which cannot be grown in the open in gardens with cool summers and significant summer rainfall. These are plants for specialists with the enthusiasm and time to lavish upon them but, given the relatively simple equipment of an unheated glasshouse or frame, there is an enormous amount of fun and pleasure to be had in trying to grow these exciting bulbs.

Above: The specialist bulbs grow well, and supply endless enjoyment, in pots in an unheated glasshouse.

Opposite: Raised beds, such as this one in the author's garden, are an excellent way of growing bulbs in poorly-drained soils.

Cape bulbs

For those gardening in mild winter areas a further realm of the bulb world opens up – that of the Cape bulbs, which originate from the predominantly winter-rainfall region of the south-west Cape of South Africa. These behave in exactly the same way as the Mediterranean and Middle Eastern bulbs, starting into growth in autumn and dying down in summer, but they are less hardy. Those who live in colder-winter areas will need to grow them in a glasshouse or conservatory with a minimal amount of heat, just enough to provide frost protection on cold nights. With that proviso, they are very simple to cultivate and will provide enormous scope and pleasure, since there are so many of

them to choose from. The chapter on Cape Bulbs gives an introduction to just a selection of those that are, or are becoming, available. If the 'bug bites', the possibilities for making a collection of these fascinating bulbs are almost endless!

Tropical bulbs

The heated conservatory is one of the great growth industries in regions that experience cold winters – extending the home into the garden, or the garden into the home, depending upon one's view! A warm glasshouse or conservatory opens up yet another field for the bulb enthusiast, and one that has to date been scarcely touched upon by commercial horticulture. Growing the tender and tropical bulbs can be great fun, since they are often very striking with large, brightly coloured or intensely fragrant flowers. On the whole, cultivation is not difficult, bearing in mind that many of them need a warm rest period (usually 18–25°C/65–77°F) of at least six to eight weeks to encourage flower bud formation. With a little searching, quite a number of tropical bulbs can be found in catalogues, and the chapter on Tender and Tropical bulbs introduces some of the more exotic ones for container cultivation in the 'extra room'.

Bulbs in containers

Container gardening has become extremely popular during the last few decades, perhaps brought about by a combination of increasingly small gardens and the great interest in that useful and potentially very attractive garden feature, the patio. Bulbs are particularly valuable for use in containers and window boxes, since they start the season very early, long before most perennials and shrubs, and can then be removed or overplanted with other subjects for the summer months right through to the first frosts. Almost any bulbs can be grown in containers and they are an attractive way of providing colour throughout the year for those with small gardens or even just a window box.

Almost any container will suffice, provided it is not too shallow. Most bulbs need to be covered by at least 5–10 cm (2–4 in) of soil (see the section on planting depths on page 135), with another 20–25 cm (8–10 in) beneath, so pots at least 25 cm (10 in) deep should be chosen. There are a few exceptions. *Cyclamen*, for example, will perform perfectly well with their tubers only just covered, and the excellent little summer-flowering *Rhodohypoxis* are ideal for quite shallow pans and troughs, although close attention needs to be paid to watering in summer.

Before planting, the bottom of the container needs some broken crocks or tiles placed over the drainage holes to prevent the soil falling through, then a good layer of well-rotted organic matter, which will give the delving roots some extra nourishment after they have grown down

through the potting soil, and will help to act as a reservoir for moisture. The soil should be an open mix that drains well and, for containers that are planted up for one season only, any of the proprietary composts will suffice. For long-term plantings, where a container or trough garden is planted with a range of alpines, bulbs or small shrubs, a loam-based mix is best, since this will retain a good structure for longer. A suitable mix is 1 part loam:

1 part peat (leafmould or coir): 1 part coarse sand, enriched with a general, balanced fertilizer at the rate recommended by the manufacturer. Later on, when the bulbs are in growth, feeds with a liquid fertilizer (preferably one designed for tomatoes, with a high potash content) are beneficial because of the restricted volume of soil available. Planting times and depths are the same as for open ground, but it often gives a better effect if bulbs are planted close together, particularly in the case of small, early-spring bulbs.

To extend the season of interest for as long as possible it is wise to choose a range of subjects that complement each other. For example, the very early dwarf chionodoxas and scillas are excellent for planting with the taller *greigii* and *kaufmanniana* tulips, which will grow up slightly later and flower in mid spring. There are many possibilities for experimentation, but it is best to avoid those bulbs that prefer cool growing conditions and a little extra moisture in the soil, such as snowdrops (*Galanthus*), snowflakes (*Leucojum*) and dog's tooth violets (*Erythronium*), since containers can get too hot and dry for them in the summer. It is also better not to mix autumn/winter/spring bulbs with summer-growing ones, since the summer growers will requiring watering at a time when the others are dormant and need to be drier, and vice versa.

For the summer months, lilies are superb container plants and, in areas where they do not thrive in the open garden, this is a very good way of growing them. As a rough guide, the larger trumpet lilies, such as 'African Queen' and *L. regale*, can be

Left: Tender bulbs like this *Stenomesson* **(Urceolina) need rather more attention than their hardier cousins but are very rewarding.**

Opposite top: The Cape bulbs, such as this fragrant *Gladiolus tristis*, **need frost protection but are otherwise very easy to cultivate. Bottom: A retaining wall in the author's garden, built to provide planting space for bulbs and rock plants.**

planted three to a 25–30 cm (10–12 in) diameter container. Even in dry weather, watering is best not carried out every day, since they dislike being permanently damp at the roots; it is preferable to allow them almost to dry out, then give them a good soak.

Another great benefit of growing bulbs in containers is that the garden can be moved! While in flower, provided they are not too large and heavy, bulbs can be placed in a prominent position, perhaps adjacent to another plant for the purposes of creating a pleasing association, then moved away again after flowering to a less conspicuous spot. Alternatively, the less expensive bulbs can be regarded as expendable, and be removed after flowering and replaced with something else, so this can really be a very versatile form of gardening. We are fortunate that, today, there is a tremendous range of containers available, varying in size, shape and material, so it is really just a case of choosing the one that is aesthetically most pleasing for a particular purpose and will also suit the pocket, for some are very expensive. One point to bear in mind is that although terracotta pots often look far more desirable than plastic ones, the latter retain moisture much better, a point worthy of consideration if a holiday away from gardening is contemplated!

25

BULBS RULE:
THE SPRING DISPLAY

The height of the bulb year is in spring, starting with snowdrops and crocuses and continuing through a range of daffodils to the later tulips and alliums. Various types can be interplanted to create a display for several months until the summer perennials and shrubs begin to flower. The best effect is created when spring bulbs are associated with other plants, but they can also be used alone to create striking bedding displays, then removed as soon as they have finished flowering to make room for new plantings. However, in perennial and shrub borders, or in grass, the bulbs should be left to die down naturally, then the dead foliage cleared away; if the leaves are removed while green, the bulbs will be weakened.

Left: Erythroniums and *Anemone nemorosa* enjoy the same semi-shaded conditions.

Right: *Crocus sieberi tricolor* does well in dappled shade with hellebores.

Right: *Anemone blanda* provides interest when the winter heathers are nearing the end of their display.

Opposite: The many varieties of wood anemone, *Anemone nemorosa***, are superb for the dappled shade. This is 'Vestal', growing with** *Dicentra.*

BULBS FOR THE SPRING

Anemone

To many gardeners anemones are the indispensable perennial species such as *A. hupehensis*, but there are some valuable tuberous ones, the most famous of which are the Mediterranean poppy anemones *A. coronaria* and *A. pavonina*, the ancestors of the florists' De Caen and St Brigid types. I have also included two of the lovely wood anemones, *A. nemorosa* and *A. ranunculoides*, which have long fleshy rhizomes. These, and *A. blanda* and *A. apennina*, thrive best in dappled shade in a humus-rich soil, whereas the poppy anemones require warm, sunny situations. These are all best planted in the autumn, although stored tubers of the florists' varieties are also offered for sale in spring for flowering later on in summer.

Associations: The wood anemones creep around to form sizeable patches and are ideal for a natural effect under and between deciduous shrubs with other perennials such as hellebores. *A. blanda* does well in a range of situations, but one of my favourite combinations is with winter heathers, *Erica carnea*. I have some white anemones adjacent to pink heathers, which are just coming to the end of their flowering season as the anemones take over; both will grow on alkaline soils.

A. blanda

A lovely and popular dwarf anemone only 5–10 cm (2–4 in) in height with attractively divided leaves overtopped by flat flowers 3–4 cm (1¼–1½ in) in diameter, with ten to twenty petals in shades of blue, pink and magenta or white. Named varieties are available, including 'White Splendour', 'Atrocaerulea' (deep blue), 'Rosea' and 'Charmer' (both pink), and 'Radar' (magenta). *A. apennina* is very similar in appearance but has a creeping rootstock unlike the rounded knobbly tubers of *A. blanda*; it is up to 15 cm (6 in) in height, usually with blue flowers, but a good white is also available. Southern Europe, but *A. blanda* extends to the Balkans and Turkey.

A. coronaria

The poppy anemone has provided us with the familiar St Brigid and De Caen varieties, which are available throughout the year as cut flowers in single or semi-double forms in a wide range of colours – red, blue, white and violet – with a dark mass of stamens in the centre. They grow to about 15–25 cm (6–10 in) in height, the flowers held above parsley-like leaves. Closely related is *A. pavonina*, which is similar but the leaves are less divided; the St Bavo anemones, also useful for cutting, have been raised from this species. The gaudy *A.* × *fulgens* has brilliant scarlet flowers, either with a few broad petals or with many narrow ones in 'Multipetala'. Mediterranean region.

A. nemorosa

The wood anemones require cool woodland conditions and are charming for naturalizing. They have creeping rhizomes producing 10–15 cm (4–6 in) stems, each with a solitary flower 2.5–4 cm (1–1½ in) across with five to eight petals, held over a whorl of ferny leaves. The wild form is normally white-flowered but there are many selections, such as 'Allenii', 'Robinsoniana' and 'Blue Bonnet' (blue), 'Alba Plena' (double white) and 'Vestal' (white with a central boss of many small petals). *A. ranunculoides* is very like this in character but has smaller, bright yellow flowers 1.5–2 cm (⅝–¾ in) across; 'Superba' is a larger-flowered form and 'Pleniflora' ('Flore Pleno') has many more petals. The hybrid between these two species, known as *A.* × *lipsiensis* (*A.* × *seemannii*), has soft sulphur-cream flowers, accompanied by

bronze-coloured leaves. These two species are widespread in Europe.

Arum

The curious Lords and Ladies or Cuckoo Pints have distinctive sail- or cowl-like spathes enclosing an erect pencil-like spadix, which bears tiny flowers hidden from view inside the tube of the spathe; these are often followed by clusters of red berries in summer or autumn. Arum tubers are planted in autumn in a semi-shaded or sunny position in any ordinary garden soil and will form clumps that can be lifted and divided in autumn or in late spring while the old leaves are still visible.

Associations: These modest plants have most impact if there are few competing plants. The showiest is the yellow *A. creticum*, and I have this growing by a bay tree, which provides a deep green neutral background; both are to be found in Crete, so the combination is appropriate!

A. creticum

An attractive species with deep green arrow-shaped leaves produced in autumn, accompanied in mid spring by 8–15 cm (3⅛–6 in) long narrow yellow spathes, which are often twisted and recurved, leaving the spadix protruding prominently. Unlike many species, this is fragrant. Crete.

A. dioscoridis

By way of contrast, this arum, 25–30 cm (10–12 in) tall, has a disgusting smell, so exceptionally awful that it is worth having as a curiosity! The leaves are plain green but the upright spathes are beautifully blotched, dark purple on a pale green or velvety-purple ground colour. Eastern Mediterranean.

A. italicum

This is also mentioned in the winter section, since it is such a good foliage plant for that time of year, with its wonderfully ornamental creamy-veined and marbled leaves. It grows to a height of 25–30 cm (10–12 in). The spathes appear in late spring, rather unexciting and pale green, but may be followed by showy spikes of red berries in summer and autumn. Europe, North Africa, western Asia.

Brimeura

Although this is far from showy, it is worth while growing *B. amethystina* for its small but brilliant blue flowers, almost into early summer. It needs cool, dappled shade where its bulbs will not get sun-baked during their summer dormancy. Bulbs are available in autumn and should be planted in a humus-rich soil.

Associations: This is a good companion for shade-loving perennials such as the attractive Japanese variegated fern *Athyrium niponicum* 'Pictum' and the smaller-leaved hostas like the blue-grey 'Hadspen Heron', flowering at a time when these are just coming into growth.

B. amethystina (Hyacinthus amethystinus)

This has a few narrow basal leaves and a 15–20 cm (6–8 in) stem with a raceme of several pendent blue tubular bells 1–1.5 cm (½–⅝ in) long, resembling a miniature English bluebell. There is also a white form, 'Alba'. Pyrenees.

Brodiaea

Brodiaeas are among the last of the spring bulbs to flower, almost into summer, but they are not summer bulbs in that their corms need to be planted in the autumn and they die down in mid to late summer. They are very similar to triteleias (see page 58) and the latter are often referred to as brodiaeas. They have wiry stems crowned by umbels of starry or funnel-shaped flowers, carried on slender stalks radiating out like the spokes of an umbrella. Although not dramatic, a clump of these can make an attractive display in a sunny border, just before the main flush of summer perennials.

Associations: I have tried these amid grey-leaved plants such as helichrysums and lavenders in an open sunny bed and the combination is really quite effective when the blue brodiaeas are in flower.

B. californica

A handsome species 25–45 cm (10–18 in) tall with loose umbels up to 20 cm (8 in) in diameter. The funnel-shaped flowers are 3–4.5 cm (1¼–1¾ in) long, usually in shades of lavender or purple with a darker vein along the centre of each of the six lobes. California.

Bulbocodium

This is not a showy plant and is mainly of interest to bulb enthusiasts, although when seen close to, the flowers are attractive, like small colchicums. The corms are planted in autumn in an open situation in gritty soil, where they will dry out somewhat during their summer dormancy.

Associations: Being dwarf, companion plantings must be chosen carefully so as not to crowd out the bulbocodiums; small alpines such as carpeting *Phlox douglasii* and prostrate thymes are suitable, and enjoy similar conditions in full sun with good drainage.

B. vernum

The bright pinkish-purple funnel-shaped flowers are about 3–4 cm (1¼–1½ in) across, almost resting on the ground. At flowering time in mid spring there are two or three short, narrow leaves which elongate later. European mountains.

Calochortus

(Mariposa Lily, Globe Lily, Fairy Lantern, Cat's Ears)

These are probably the most striking of all North American bulbs, equalling or exceeding the tulips in gaudiness. They are mostly fairly tall, slender plants with long, narrow basal leaves and pendent globe-like to erect saucer-shaped flowers; these are made up of three large showy inner petals and three smaller outer ones, usually with contrasting zones of colour in the centre and sometimes lined with hairs. In colder, damper areas they need to be given some protection, either from severe frosts in winter or from excess rain while they are dormant in summer. In such places it is therefore best to grow them in pots in cold frames or a frost-free glasshouse, where they can be very rewarding in late spring to early summer. The bulbs are planted in autumn in a well-drained soil, and then are nearly dried out in mid to late summer when they have died down.

Associations: For those with a suitable climate it is worth trying calochortus among ornamental grasses – a natural association for some of the species, and the grasses offer some support for the slender stems. I have succeeded with *C. albus* in a heather bed, the heathers affording some protection in winter, some support for the stems when in flower and help in drying out the soil in summer. The effect was also good!

C. albus

One of the smaller species, this has 15–25 cm (6–10 in) stems carrying several pendent white or reddish-flushed globe-shaped flowers about 2–3 cm (¾ –1¼ in) in diameter. *C. amabilis* is very like this but the flowers are deep yellow. Both are from California.

C. luteus

A spectacular plant, 25–35 cm (10–14 in) in height, with branched stems carrying several wide-open bright yellow flowers 5–6 cm (2–2½ in) across, facing upwards and usually marked with brown in the centre. California.

C. splendens

This is similar to *C. luteus* in the shape and size of its flowers, but they are pale lavender-purple, usually with darker purple markings in the hairy centre, borne on stems up to 60 cm (2 ft) in height. There are several related species with the same overall appearance, although differing subtly, mainly in the shape of the nectaries at the bases of the larger petals; in *C. splendens* the nectary is roughly circular. *C. superbus* has white, yellow or lavender flowers, often yellow in the centre with brown or purple markings and with an inverted V-shaped nectary. In *C. venustus* the nectary is quadrangular and the flowers may be white, yellow, orange, pink or lavender to mahogany red, often darker in the centre and with a red-brown blotch on each petal. *C. vestae* is quite like *C. splendens* but the nectary is crescent-shaped. All from California.

C. uniflorus

Although not impressive, this is still a delightful plant, some 10–25 cm (4–10 in) tall with several upward-facing, saucer-shaped flowers, 4–5 cm (1½–2 in) across, in soft lilac with a darker violet blotch on each inner petal. It is a good species to start with, since it is quite easy to grow and will undoubtedly encourage further

experimentation with this lovely genus. California, Oregon.

Camassia

Although these are dealt with here in the spring-flowering section, since they grow through winter and spring, they do not flower until late spring or early summer. Unlike most spring bulbs, these are tall plants with long racemes of large starry blue, violet or creamy-white flowers, carried over long, narrow lance-shaped leaves. They are very hardy and easily cultivated in ordinary garden soil; they are, in fact, best in heavier soils that are well supplied with moisture, so they are suitable for growing amid hardy perennials, between shrubs and

in grass. The large bulbs are planted in autumn.

Associations: The long racemes of flowers of the paler forms stand out very well against dark or strongly coloured backgrounds, and it is worth planting dense clumps of bulbs for greater effect. One combination that works well is the pale blue *C. cusickii* in front of *Photinia* 'Red Robin', which has young bronze-coloured foliage at about the same time as the camassia flowers. Flowering slightly earlier than the majority of summer perennials, camassias are valuable for filling the gap between the early bulbs and the later herbaceous border subjects.

C. cusickii

Growing to 1 m (3¼ ft) or more in height, this is a stately plant with grey-green basal leaves and long stiff racemes of pale blue flowers about 3–5 cm (1¼–2 in) across. North America.

C. leichtlinii

This is a robust plant up to 1.5 m (5 ft) in height. The long racemes carry many 6–8 cm (2½–3⅛ in) diameter flowers varying from deep to mid violet-blue or white. The cream-white form is known as 'Alba' and there is a double version with many narrow creamy petals, 'Semiplena'. North America.

The North American camassias prefer moist soils. Here, *C. cusickii* and hostas are growing with a backdrop of *Photinia* 'Red Robin'.

Right: The very early glory of the snow, *Chionodoxa luciliae*, planted with *Euphorbia myrsinites*.

Opposite: The bronzy foliage of a sedge, *Carex buchananii*, acts as a foil for a red form of *Corydalis solida*.

C. quamash
At 20–40 cm (8–16 in), this is a shorter, more slender plant with variable pale to deep violet-blue or white flowers 3–6 cm (1½–2½ in) across. It looks good in grass, but the leaves stay well into the summer, hindering mowing until later on. North America.

Chionodoxa

These small early-spring bulbs are excellent for naturalizing, since they will take dappled shade under deciduous shrubs and produce large crops of seeds. They have short racemes of flattish blue or lilac flowers, which are individually larger than those of their relatives, the scillas. They are neat plants, each bulb producing only two basal leaves at ground level. The small bulbs are planted in autumn, fairly close together (2–4 cm/¾–1½ in) to provide a mass effect.

Associations: Chionodoxas grow well among the roots of deciduous shrubs and can be quite successful at brightening the bottom of a hedge in early spring. They can be used for providing early colour in containers planted with later bulbs such as tulips, thus extending the flowering season; blue chionodoxas with dwarf scarlet tulips, such as *T. greigii* 'Red Riding Hood', work well.

C. luciliae (C. gigantea)
There is much confusion between this and the next species, but it should have rather large pale lavender-blue flowers, up to three on each stem and facing upwards. Turkey.

C. sardensis

Although similar to *C. siehei*, with several flowers per stem, these are slightly smaller and bluer than either of the other two. Turkey.

C. siehei (*C. luciliae* of gardens and many catalogues)

This is the most frequently seen species in gardens, with several smaller purple-blue flowers with a distinct white eye in the centre, facing outwards rather than upwards. There is a white-flowered form, 'Alba', and a very vigorous pink, 'Pink Giant'. Turkey.

× **Chionoscilla**

These are hybrids between chionodoxas and *Scilla bifolia* and closely resemble the latter. The planting time and conditions are as described for *Chionodoxa*.

Associations: These hybrids are vigorous and will grow happily among robust perennials such as pulmonarias and hellebores; their very early strong-blue flowers are excellent in association with the silvery-marbled leaves of the *Pulmonaria longifolia* and *P. saccharata* varieties.

× *C. allenii*

Like its parents, this has a pair of leaves and 10–15 cm (4–6 in) stems bearing several starry flowers in one-sided racemes, each flower about 2.5 cm (1 in) across in variable shades of rich violet-blue. There are named selections but they are seldom available. Garden hybrid.

Colchicum

The main entry for these predominantly autumn-flowering plants will be found on page 93 of the autumn section, but we must not forget that there are several attractive small-flowered spring species, with elegant little flowers produced at the same time as the leaves. The corms are planted in autumn in open sunny situations that will dry out in summer. In view of their size, it is preferable to grow them in pots where they can be viewed and appreciated more closely.

Associations: If planted outside, these are best among dwarf alpines such as *Dianthus*, small *Erysimum* varieties, saxifrages and carpeting plants.

C. hungaricum

A most attractive little plant and one of the best of all the spring-flowering species, with two lance-shaped, hairy-margined leaves and small goblet-like white or lilac-pink flowers with dark stamens, usually only 5–8 cm (2–3⅛ in) high. Balkans.

C. luteum

Unique in that it is the only yellow colchicum, this is only 5–10 cm (2–4 in) in height at flowering time and has short, glossy green leaves accompanying bright yellow funnel-shaped flowers, sometimes with a bronze tint on the outside. Central Asia, western Himalayas.

Corydalis

The fumitories are interesting plants related to the poppies, although their flowers are quite different in having a two-lipped appearance with a conspicuous spur. Many *Corydalis* are not tuberous-rooted, but there are quite a lot of spring-flowering species that do have tubers and these are normally grouped together with 'bulbs' in nursery catalogues. They are elegant little plants with short racemes of flowers accompanied by grey-green ferny leaves. The tubers are dormant in summer and are planted in early autumn in a humus-rich soil in dappled shade, where they will not become too hot and dry in summer, since their tubers can shrivel.

Associations: The common purple *Corydalis solida* is excellent for naturalizing under deciduous trees and shrubs, and between early perennials such as hellebores. The pink and red selections are just as easy to please, but in view of their greater cost it is better to choose positions where they can be appreciated individually, for instance among dwarf shrubs and small rhododendrons that will flower slightly later.

C. ambigua

The lovely intense blue fumitory in cultivation under this name should perhaps, due to confusion in gardens, be called *C. fumariifolia*. It is 10–20 cm (4–8 in) in height with racemes of long-spurred flowers, variable in intensity and some forms being a more purple-blue. It needs a cool position, such as a 'peat garden', although leafmould is a more suitable source of humus. Eastern Asia.

C. bulbosa (C. cava)

An old favourite, long cultivated as a woodland plant for naturalizing, this has racemes of dull purple flowers over dissected green leaves. There is a very nice white form, 'Alba', with dark purple bracts amid the flowers. Europe.

C. caucasica 'Alba'

This is a superb hardy plant, which will seed itself around when growing happily in a well-drained humus-rich soil. It should be referred to as *C. malkensis*, but either name may be found in catalogues at present. It is about 10–15 cm (4–6 in) in height with racemes of long-spurred white flowers, which are distinctive in having a large lower lip, giving the flower a very substantial appearance. Caucasus.

C. solida

Arguably this is the most satisfactory of the tuberous corydalis, very easy to cultivate and extremely variable in flower colour, so that a lot of fun can be had in selecting different forms. It is about 10–15 cm (4–6 in) in height with racemes of curved-spurred flowers in shades of purple, red or pink through to white, accompanied by ferny grey-green foliage. The most showy selection is 'George Baker' ("transylvanica"), with deep glowing red flowers, but equally attractive is the pale pink 'Beth Evans'. Europe.

Crocus

I am biased on the subject of crocuses, having studied them botanically for ten years and written a book on them, but I think all will agree that they are an essential component of the spring garden. Bored colleagues have suggested that there are really only three crocuses – one blue, one yellow and one white – but there are, in fact, over eighty species! For garden display purposes, many of these can be discounted since they are really collectors' items for cosseting, but several of them are first-rate garden plants and I have picked out a few that I think are sufficiently different to merit planting. The corms are offered in autumn and should be planted fairly soon after purchase, since they start to root quite early. All those mentioned are suitable for a well-drained soil and most are best in full sun, since the flowers will not open properly if grown in shade; but in areas with very hot summers, dappled shade may be preferable, since the dormant corms can become over-dried. They grow to a height of 5–10 cm (2–4 in).

Associations: With so much variation in colour there are many possibilities for experimental companion plantings. Crocuses look wonderful in grass and for those that grow well in these conditions – such as the *C. vernus* cultivars and the more vigorous hybrids of *C. chrysanthus* – there is no better way, and they seem to be less liable to mouse attack than those in bare ground. Their bright starry flowers are also enhanced by the ornamental grasses, and I have been encouraged by the results of small-scale plantings of white or blue crocuses among the smaller stipas and grey *Festuca glauca*.

C. ancyrensis

This is one of the smaller-flowered species, but has several flowers per corm (it is often advertised as 'Golden Bunch') and they are of a bright orange-yellow. Turkey.

C. angustifolius (C. susianus)

Although very similar to *C. ancyrensis*, the flowers are larger and have dark bronze stripes or staining outside. In bright sun they open out wide and the petals reflex. Crimea.

C. biflorus and C. chrysanthus

I have put these two together since they have been hybridized to produce many excellent garden plants referred to as the

C. chrysanthus cultivars. The wild forms are fairly small-flowered, yellow or cream in *C. chrysanthus* and blue, white or purple-striped on a paler ground colour in *C. biflorus*. The hybrids are much larger and come in a great range of colours, and are very vigorous, increasing into clumps. They flower in early spring and have elegant bowl-shaped fragrant flowers. *C. biflorus* subsp. *alexandri* has striking bicoloured flowers, white inside and dark blue-violet outside; subsp. *weldenii* 'Fairy' is also white, shaded greyish-blue outside; and 'Miss Vain' is wholly white with a hint of blue near the base. Good *C. chrysanthus* cultivars include: 'Advance' (yellow inside, purplish-bronze outside), 'Blue Pearl' (light blue with yellow centre), 'Cream Beauty' (rich cream with yellow centre and orange stigmas), 'E. A. Bowles' (yellow with a bronzy-green base outside), 'Gipsy Girl' (yellow with bronze-purple stripes outside), 'Ladykiller' (white inside, stained intense violet outside), 'Snow Bunting' (pure white with a yellow centre) and 'Zwanenburg Bronze' (yellow inside and rich bronze-brown outside). There are many others and it is fun to collect them, adding a few each year. *C. biflorus* occurs wild from Italy to Iran, whereas *C. chrysanthus* comes from the Balkans and Turkey.

C. dalmaticus

A very easy crocus that will increase well into clumps. It has yellow-centred lilac flowers, silvery outside and usually veined purple. The Italian *C. etruscus* is very similar and just as accommodating in the garden. *C. dalmaticus* is from Montenegro.

C. flavus

This is the wild species from which the old favourite, the large Dutch yellow crocus 'Golden Yellow', has been bred, a vigorous hybrid between *C. flavus* and *C. angustifolius*, which is such a valuable plant for providing early splashes of colour in grass or at the front of borders, flowering at the same time as hellebores. The rich yellow flowers have a little dark veining outside and are much larger than those of the wild form of *C. flavus*. The Balkans, Turkey.

C. gargaricus

An uncommon but delightful little crocus with rounded 'tubby' deep orange flowers, which enjoys a slightly damper situation in the garden where it can form patches because of its stoloniferous (shoot-producing) habit. Turkey.

C. imperati

This is a surprising crocus, since the flowers are biscuit-coloured outside but as they open they reveal a bright purple interior. The Corsican *C. corsicus* is like a smaller version of this, very similar in colouring, and *C. minimus* from Corsica and Sardinia is even smaller; the form of the latter which is usually offered by nurseries is deep violet on the outside. *C. imperati* is from Italy.

C. korolkowii

Another bright yellow spring crocus, which has very shiny petals, as if they have been varnished. They open out flat in the sun and have a honey-like scent. The outside may be plain yellow, variously striped or suffused bronze, and several of these variations have been named, such as 'Kiss of Spring'. Central Asia.

Top: Crocuses at the Royal Botanic Gardens, Kew, part of a vast planting of *C. vernus* cultivars provided by Reader's Digest.

Bottom: Associations seen in the wild often provide good ideas for garden plantings. The Turkish *Crocus gargaricus* and *Scilla bifolia* with *Verbascum* leaves.

C. malyi

A seldom seen but excellent hardy crocus with long elegant creamy-white flowers, enlivened by a yellow centre and bright orange-red stigmas. Dalmatia.

C. sieberi

One of the best of the spring crocuses, with variable bright lilac flowers with a yellow throat. Some forms are deeper violet, for example 'Violet Queen', while 'Tricolor' has three zones of colour – a yellow centre with a white band between it and the lilac of the upper part of the petals. 'Hubert Edelsten' has near-white flowers, banded outside with lilac patterns, and 'Bowles' White' is a superb creamy-white crocus with a deep egg-yolk centre. Greece.

C. tommasinianus

Since this often flowers in late winter I have included it in the winter section on page 106.

C. vernus

This is the wild species from which all the large-flowered Dutch purple, purple-striped and white crocuses have been raised, the wild forms being seldom cultivated. The cultivars are often planted in bowls for an early display and they provide a marvellous mass effect amid grass in many parks and gardens. For this purpose, mixed collections are very cheap but named individual colours are also available. 'Jeanne d'Arc' is pure white with contrasting orange stigmas; 'Pickwick' flowers are extravagantly striped purple on a white ground; 'Remembrance' and 'Purpureus Grandiflorus' are good, deep glossy violet forms; and 'Vanguard' is

pale lavender with a silvery wash outside. European mountains.

C. versicolor

In the last century many forms of this crocus were available, but most have disappeared from cultivation. It is easily grown and highly rewarding, with white or pale purple flowers conspicuously striped purple outside and often suffused with a biscuit colour. The form known as 'Picturatus' is still offered and is white with violet veins. Southern France, northern Italy.

Cyclamen

Although most of the wild species of cyclamen are thought of as connoisseur's plants, suitable for cosseting in an unheated glasshouse where their finer details can be appreciated more closely, they are hardier than one might suspect and it is worth trying experimental plantings outside. As current President of the Cyclamen Society I feel that I should mention most of these fascinating little plants, the majority of which will be found in the autumn and winter sections. The tubers can be planted in autumn or at almost any time of the year if they are bought as growing plants, which is by far the best way to obtain them. A well-drained humus-rich soil in dappled shade is suitable, preferably in a position sheltered from cold winds. Most of them grow up to 5–10 cm (2–4 in) tall.

Associations: The spring cyclamen flower slightly after the initial flush of early bulbs and are coming up to their peak as the winter *C. coum* is going over. For this

reason it makes sense to have a cyclamen bed, incorporating several species to spread the flowering season, and including winter aconites and snowdrops, which enjoy similar conditions. Combining autumnal cyclamen will provide flowers for a long period, and their ornamental foliage lasts for six to seven months.

C. balearicum

One of the least showy, this white-flowered species makes up for its modesty by having interesting leaves, often heavily silvered, and the small flowers are fragrant. Balearic Islands.

C. libanoticum

A lovely plant with large pale pink flowers having sharply defined red marks around the mouth, and a musty fragrance. The leaves are less dramatically patterned than in most of the species. Lebanon.

C. pseudibericum

This is among the most attractive of all the cyclamen, with large showy fragrant flowers, rich carmine with a blackish-violet stain near the white-rimmed mouth. The heart-shaped leaves are often gorgeously marked with silver and green patterns and have toothed margins. Turkey.

C. repandum

I find this the best of the spring species for outdoors, since it emerges later on when the frosts are less severe. It has deep reddish-carmine flowers with elegant long petals, deliciously fragrant and accompanied by dark green leaves with lighter patterns. Slightly less frost-hardy are two variants, subsp. *rhodense* with white flowers with a pink rim around the mouth and subsp. *peloponnesiacum*, which has pink flowers, also with a darker mouth; in both of these the leaves are splashed with silver. Italy, Dalmatia, Greece and the Greek islands.

C. trochopteranthum

My favourite species, related to the winter-flowering *C. coum* but having flowers shaped like a ship's propeller, this is strongly musty-fragrant and ranges from carmine to nearly white. The heart-shaped leaves are very varied in their silvery patterns. Turkey.

Dracunculus

This is an amazing plant belonging to the arum family, with a large coloured spathe surrounding a thick pencil-like spadix, which protrudes from the mouth of the spathe and carries insignificant flowers at its base, hidden from view in the tube of the spathe. It is very striking and worth growing for interest's sake, although the spathe has a most disgusting smell. The best situation is a sheltered spot between small shrubs, where the tubers will get warm and fairly dry during the summer when dormant. They are usually offered in autumn and should be planted at this time.

Associations: Natural associations often work well, so it is worth planting *Dracunculus* between Mediterranean shrubs that enjoy hot sunny places, such as *Cistus*, *Myrtus* and the grey-blue *Euphorbia characias*.

D. vulgaris (Dragon Arum)

A vigorous plant up to 1 m (3¼ ft) in height, with a striking green-blotched stem and large, attractively lobed leaves. In late spring or early summer a large purple-maroon spathe is produced at the top of the stem, 30–45 cm (12–18 in) in length and with a protruding dark shiny maroon spadix. Mediterranean region.

Erythronium

The attractive dog's tooth violets are very distinctive, having two broad leaves at ground level, either plain green or beautifully mottled, between which arises a bare flower stem carrying one to several pendent bells, which reflex at the tips to display striking zones of colour inside. All

those mentioned below are suitable for a cool, humus-rich soil (leafmould is better than peat) in dappled shade, where they can be left undisturbed. With a good humus content they can grow satisfactorily on alkaline soils as well as acid; the European *E. dens-canis* is more lime-tolerant than the North American species. The canine tooth-shaped bulbs are obtainable in autumn and are best planted fairly deeply, with about 8 cm (3⅛ in) of soil above the tip. Flowering takes place after the main flush of early spring bulbs, but before the taller tulips come into their own.

Associations: These are ideal subjects for planting beneath and between deciduous trees and shrubs, although I have also seen excellent drifts of *E. revolutum* between evergreen rhododendrons; and I have a clump of yellow *E. tuolumnense* growing well in the roots of a bay tree, where it shows up beautifully against the strong green of the bay leaves.

E. americanum

One of the smaller, less significant species but well worth planting in an area where it can be left to form patches, since it increases by stolons. The leaves are beautifully brown-and-green mottled and the solitary yellow flowers are suffused bronze on the outside. Eastern North America.

One of the best of all the dog's tooth violets, *Erythronium hendersonii*, originally from northern California and southern Oregon. Here it is seen growing with grape hyacinths in dappled shade.

E. californicum

This is one of the best of all, with attractively brown-marbled lance-shaped leaves and stems up to 30 cm (12 in) tall, carrying large elegant creamy-white flowers that have a ring of rusty-coloured markings in the centre. The selection known as 'White Beauty' is excellent, since it increases freely by offsets from the tubers, forming dense floriferous clumps. California.

E. dens-canis

The European dog's tooth violet is rather earlier and shorter than most of the American species, and has elliptical leaves, beautifully mottled brown and bluish-green. The stem is only 5–10 cm (2–4 in) in height and carries a single flower, which may be rose, pinkish-lilac, carmine or white with yellow, brown or purple zones in the centre. Several have been named as cultivars, including 'Frans Hals' (purple with greenish centre), 'Rose Queen' (pinkish-lilac) and 'Snowflake' (pure white). *E. caucasicum* is overall very similar to *E. dens-canis* but has creamy-white flowers with brownish speckling in the centre. *E. dens-canis* is European and *E. caucasicum* from the Caucasus mountains.

E. hendersonii

I regard this as one of the most beautiful species, easy to cultivate although tending to stay as single plants rather than forming clumps like *E. californicum* 'White Beauty' and *E. tuolumnense*. It has mottled lance-shaped leaves and stems up to 30 cm (12 in) carrying up to ten lilac flowers, marked with a deep purple eye in the centre. California, Oregon.

E. oregonum

This robust species has mottled leaves and stems up to 30 cm (12 in) tall carrying up to five large white flowers with conspicuous zigzag brown markings and yellow zones in the centre. The stamens are yellow, whereas those of the similar *E. californicum* are white. Oregon, Washington and Vancouver Island.

E. revolutum

For long-term naturalizing this is probably the best of all since, when thriving, it will seed itself freely and flowers very reliably. The leaves are gorgeously mottled with brown, contrasting with the large deep-pink flowers, which have a yellow zone in their centres. California, north to Vancouver Island.

E. tuolumnense

This very easily cultivated *Erythronium* soon increases into clumps. The large leaves are plain shiny green, overtopped by 25–35 cm (10–14 in) stems carrying up to four bright yellow flowers. California.

Erythronium hybrids

Several hybrids are now offered, crosses between *E. tuolumnense*, *E. californicum* and *E. oregonum*, all having yellow flowers and slightly mottled foliage. 'Citronella', 'Jeannine' and 'Pagoda' are good garden plants that increase well into clumps, especially 'Pagoda'. 'Jeannine' has slightly larger, deeper yellow flowers, and 'Pagoda' is the palest, a soft sulphur-yellow.

Fritillaria

Although many fritillaries have subdued green, brown and purple colours, their pendent bells are very elegant and add a touch of the unusual to the garden. There are many species, currently very popular with bulb enthusiasts, but only a few are suitable for the open garden, the smaller ones being better in pots where they can be appreciated in more detail. Most 'outdoor' fritillaries prefer well-drained soil in open or slightly shaded situations that partially dry out in summer, so they can be planted in borders with shrubs and perennials; but

Above: *Erythronium* **'Pagoda' with the wood spurge** *Euphorbia amygdaloides* **'Purpurea'.**

Opposite: Snake's head fritillaries, *F. meleagris*, in a cool position with dog's tooth violets, scillas and dwarf rhododendrons.

the well-known *F. meleagris*, and
F. camschatcensis, prefer damper situations
and the former will naturalize in damp
grassland. The bulbs are planted in
autumn, as early as possible since some of
them, and notably the crown imperials,
start to root in late summer.

Associations: The two that are most
frequently cultivated are *F. meleagris* and
F. imperialis, both wonderful garden plants
but requiring different situations.
F. meleagris looks at its best when growing
in grass, its natural habitat, but make sure
that there are plenty of white ones
intermixed, since these stand out much
better than the pinkish ones and attract the
eye. They also do well among dwarf
rhododendrons and other shrubs. The very
striking crown imperial *F. imperialis* needs
to be placed where it will receive plenty of
sun and a warm, dryish summer while
dormant. Large plantings are not necessary
for a good effect; a few bulbs of the yellow
form look marvellous with the grey leaves
and powdery blue flowers of the rosemary
'Miss Jessopp's Upright', or with the white
form of honesty, *Lunaria annua*. Beth
Chatto has some wonderful plantings of
the orange-red form near the ornamental
purple-leafed version of New Zealand flax,
Phormium tenax, a highly effective
combination.

F. acmopetala

A slender species 15–35 cm (6–14 in) tall
with scattered narrow greyish leaves and
one or two pale green, brown-stained bells
3–4 cm (1¼–1½ in) long, which have
elegantly reflexed tips. Turkey.

F. affinis (F. lanceolata)

A very variable species from 15–100 cm
(6 in–3¼ ft) in height with whorls of leaves
and 2–4 cm (¾–1½ in) long bells, which
may be purple or green with a tessellated
(mosaic) pattern, sometimes solitary,
sometimes with several in a raceme.
Western North America.

F. biflora

This fairly small species is best known for
the selection 'Martha Roderick', named
after the mother of Californian plantsman
Wayne Roderick, who discovered it. It is
usually 15–20 cm (6–8 in) in height with
glossy green leaves clustered near the base
and 3–4 cm (1¼–1½ in) long bells, which
are brown with white patches near the tips.
Also known as *F. roderickii*. California.

F. camschatcensis (Black Sarana)

This fascinating plant prefers cooler,
moister growing conditions than most and
may be grown in a humus-rich soil with
rhododendrons. Its 15–50 cm (6–20 in)
stems have whorls of glossy green leaves
and several blackish-chocolate bells 2–3 cm
(¾–1¼ in) long. Eastern Asia, north-west
North America.

F. crassifolia

One of the many greenish-flowered species
with up to three bells 2–3 cm (¾–1¼ in)
long, usually chequered brown. It is fairly
short at about 10–20 cm (4–8 in) tall,
with scattered, often twisted, greyish leaves.
There are many different forms in
cultivation. Turkey, Iran, Iraq.

F. graeca

This may be anything from 5 to 20 cm
(2–8 in) tall with scattered grey-green leaves
and from one to four wide bells 2–3 cm
(¾–1¼ in) long, green and brown tessellated
and marked with a smart green band on
the outside of each petal. Greece.

F. imperialis (Crown Imperial)

By far the most impressive species, this has
been popular for centuries as a garden plant.
It will grow to 1.5 m (5 ft) in height, with
its stems very leafy in the lower half and its
leaves an attractive glossy green and carried
in whorls. Several large, pendent widely
bell-shaped brick-orange flowers about
4.5–6 cm (1¾–2½ in) long are carried in an

Fritillaria imperialis
**'Lutea' at the château
of Saint-Jean-de-
Beauregard near**

**Paris, photographed
by courtesy of
Monsieur and
Madame de Curel.**

umbel, which is crowned by a further tuft of small leaves. The only drawback is that the whole plant has a fox-like smell. Several varieties have been named, including 'Lutea' and 'Lutea Maxima', both with large yellow bells; 'Rubra', a deep red; 'Aurora', a rich orange-red; and variegated leaf forms are sometimes available. Turkey to the Himalayas.

F. meleagris (Snake's Head Fritillary)

This is arguably the best garden fritillary of all, since it is easy to obtain and cultivate, provided that it does not get too hot and dry. It is a graceful, slender plant with scattered narrow grey-green leaves and solitary pendent bells 3–4.5 cm (1¼–1¾ in) long. Although often pinkish-purple with a striking darker tessellated pattern, there are various selections including 'Alba' and 'Aphrodite' (both white), 'Charon' (purple) and 'Saturnus', which is a deeper reddish-violet, but a good mixed collection is as effective as any. Europe.

F. michailovskyi

I have a great liking for this species, since the first live specimens to be introduced to cultivation were found in Turkey by my wife Maggie. Thanks to Dutch nurserymen, it is now available quite cheaply. It is 10–20 cm (4–8 in) tall with grey-green leaves and up to four bells 2–3 cm (¾–1¼ in) long, bicoloured purplish-brown with bright yellow tips. Turkey.

F. pallidiflora

A striking fritillary, 15–30 cm (6–12 in) tall with broad grey leaves and a raceme of up to five angular-oblong pale yellow bells, faintly chequered brown and 4–5 cm

(1½–2 in) long. This very hardy species needs cool growing conditions. Central Asia.

F. persica

A very distinctive fritillary, the 1–1.5 m (3¼–5 ft) stem is clothed with many narrow, twisted grey-green leaves and bearing a long raceme of up to twenty small conical purple, brownish or yellowish flowers, 1.5–2 cm (⅝–¾ in) long. The forms usually offered by nurseries are deep plum with a greyish overlay. A similar situation to F. imperialis is best. Middle East.

F. pontica

Although not showy, this has a quiet charm and is relatively easy to cultivate in dappled shade. It is 15–45 cm (6–18 in) in height with grey-green leaves mostly in pairs and a whorl of three at the top, standing above the pendent 3–5 cm (1¼–2 in) long bells; these are green flushed with brown without any tessellated pattern. F. involucrata is somewhat similar in having the three leaves at the apex, but the flowers are pale green or greenish-yellow, slightly tessellated brown, and the leaves are much narrower. F. pontica is from Greece and Turkey, F. involucrata from the Maritime Alps.

F. pudica

Such a beautiful little plant is well worth trying in an open sunny, gritty bed to see if you are one of the lucky ones for whom it will grow well. It is only 5–15 cm (2–6 in) tall with a few scattered greyish-green leaves and one or two buttery-yellow cone-shaped bells, which sometimes age copper-red; they are about 2.5–3 cm (1–1¼ in) long. Western North America.

F. pyrenaica (Pyrenean Fritillary)

Not a showy species, and it has an unpleasant smell, but it is easy to cultivate in semi-shade and attractive when growing in a clump. The 15–30 cm (6–12 in) stems bear narrow, scattered greyish leaves and one or two deep blackish-purple bells 2.5–4 cm (1–1½ in) long, which have reflexed tips revealing a burnished greenish-yellow interior. F. lusitanica (F. hispanica) is somewhat similar but usually an overall paler brownish or greenish colour, tessellated darker. F. lusitanica is from Spain and Portugal, F. pyrenaica from the Pyrenees.

A good clump of the blackish Fritillaria pyrenaica, an interesting plant for the perennial border.

Right: For naturalizing in dappled shade there are few better spring bulbs than the English bluebell, *Hyacinthoides non-scripta*.

Opposite: Hyacinth cultivars can be planted out after forcing indoors and make good, long-lasting garden plants.

F. uva-vulpis ('F. assyriaca')

A small, slender fritillary up to 25 cm (10 in) in height with erect glossy green leaves, bearing one to two small dusky greyish-purple bells 1.5–2.5 cm (⅝–1 in) long with contrasting yellow tips. It does well in a sharply drained bed, increasing into clumps. Turkey, Iraq.

F. verticillata

A fascinating plant with slender stems up to 60 cm (2 ft) with whorls of narrow leaves that have tendril-like tips. The variant usually seen is var. *thunbergii* (*F. thunbergii*), which has a raceme of several conical bells 2.5–3.5 cm (1–1⅜ in) long, creamy white with a greenish tessellated pattern. It should not be planted where it will get hot and dry, but otherwise is relatively easy to cultivate. East Asia.

Hermodactylus

This is better known as *Iris tuberosa* and is just like a small iris, although with rather strange flower colours and curious misshapen tubers. Its leaves are long and narrow, square in cross-section like those of *I. reticulata*. Occasionally it is seen on sale as a cut flower. The tubers should be planted in autumn in a warm sunny situation where they will dry in summer, otherwise they will not flower well. Although the best colonies seem to be associated with alkaline soils, it can be successful on light sandy soils and, when doing well, will spread to form large patches, flowering in mid spring.

Associations: Its liking for warm sunny situations makes this a good companion for other Mediterranean plants such as *Iris unguicularis*, *Cistus* and *Convolvulus cneorum* in a position where it will not be disturbed by cultivation.

H. tuberosus (Widow Iris)

The fragrant iris-shaped flowers are carried singly on 15–30 cm (6–12 in) stems and are about 4–5 cm (1½–2 in) across, greenish-yellow or straw colour and marked at the tips of the three larger petals with a blackish-brown velvety patch. Mediterranean region.

Hyacinthoides

For those who do not recognize the name, these are the bluebells that have also been known as scillas and *Endymion*. Although somewhat despised by some English gardeners, since these are native plants that can be a pest, they are lovely for partially shaded areas under and between deciduous shrubs. They will tolerate quite damp heavy soils and in fact will not thrive in hot, dry situations. The bulbs should be planted in autumn and are then best left undisturbed to form clumps for a mass effect.

Associations: One of the best plantings I have seen of the English bluebell was a drift of it in combination with the white allium, *A. ursinum*, but of course both of these can be pests, so they should be confined to areas where they can be allowed to form colonies. The larger Spanish bluebell is good for bringing late spring colour to borders to fill the gap between the early pulmonarias and hellebores and the main flush of summer perennials.

H. hispanica

A very robust bluebell up to 40 cm (16 in) in height with broad glossy strap-like leaves and racemes of blue, pink or white bells. Unlike the English bluebell, this raceme does not nod over at the apex and the flowers are more widely bell-shaped. Iberian Peninsula, North Africa.

H. non-scripta

The English bluebell is a more slender plant with narrower bells carried in a one-sided raceme, which has a nodding apex. There are blue, pink and white forms. Western Europe.

Hyacinthus

The Turkish *Hyacinthus orientalis* was a popular plant, centuries ago, with the Ottoman Turks, who selected many varieties – even doubles – and left coloured drawings of them as proof of their expertise. Hyacinths have been popular ever since for their early, highly fragrant flowers, especially indoors in bowls, but they are equally good as garden plants and, once they have settled in, the bulbs will last for many years. They do well in any reasonably well-drained soil in sun or slight shade and can survive quite dry conditions at the bottom of a hedge or under shrubs. Planted permanently in the garden, the flower spikes are never as dense as they are in their first year after purchase, but they remain just as showy and fragrant and perhaps

rather more elegant. For those who prefer the smaller-flowered types there are the Multiflora, Roman and Cynthella hyacinths, which are more akin to the wild species in appearance. The bulbs are on sale in early autumn and should be planted soon after they are obtained. For indoor use in bowls they should be planted and watered, then kept cool outdoors to encourage root growth. If intended for winter-flowering (for Christmas in the Northern Hemisphere), only 'prepared' bulbs should be obtained; these are potted about twelve weeks before the proposed flowering time to give enough time for good roots to form, then warmed progressively during the forcing stage. For outdoor plantings, buy the cheaper bulbs sold as bedding hyacinths.

Associations: Planted outdoors, hyacinths are good perennials, flowering in mid spring. The great range of colours available means that various colour combinations with other plants can be tried. Pink varieties such as 'Anna Marie' go very well with grey-leaved plants – I had a clump for many years growing in the roots of an old rosemary bush to great effect – and soft blue or white would be equally attractive. For formal bedding schemes, the winter/spring violas flower at the same time as hyacinths, so, yet again, there is plenty of scope for experimentation; blue hyacinths and creamy-white violas work well together.

H. orientalis

The wild form has a cluster of narrow basal leaves and 10–25 cm (4–10 in) stems carrying loose racemes of blue, rarely pink or white, tubular flowers 2–3 cm (¾–1¼ in) long, with six elegantly recurved lobes. Turkey, Syria.

Hyacinthus cultivars

There are many large-flowered hyacinth cultivars to select from, single and double, so the following is just a small representative selection:

Large-flowered

'Anna Marie' – pink, darkening with age; fairly stocky plants
'Blue Magic' – purple-violet, whitish in the centre
'City of Haarlem' – soft primose yellow
'Delft Blue' – soft lilac-blue
'Distinction' – deep maroon-purple, like beetroot
'Gipsy Queen' – salmon and apricot
'Jan Bos' – rich red
'White Pearl' – pure white with yellow stamens

Double

'Hollyhock' – deep crimson, each flower tightly double

Multiflora

'Blue Princess', 'Pink Princess' and 'White Princess' have several stems per bulb, the flowers are more widely spaced and are individually smaller than in the above varieties.

Ipheion

Flowering slightly after the early spring bulbs, this little onion relative is an attractive plant for sunny to partially shaded situations, preferring open light soils, where it will increase rapidly into clumps. It is less successful in cold, damp clays, and in such conditions it is necessary to add gritty sand and humus to lighten the soil. The small white bulbs are planted in early autumn, since they start to root and produce leaves long before the winter. Only one species is generally cultivated, but there are several colour forms of this that are worth seeking.

Associations: Many years ago I remember seeing a huge drift of *I. uniflorum*, the 'original' pastel blue form, growing and flowering in profusion beneath deciduous azaleas on a sunny bank, and these looked marvellous, but I have never managed to achieve success to this extent! The white form flowers at about the same time as the smaller species tulips and I have it growing

in a sunny bed with scarlet *T. linifolia* and the trailing blue-green *Euphorbia myrsinites*.

I. uniflorum

In mid spring the narrow pale green or greyish-green foliage acts as a pleasing foil for the upright starry pale blue flowers, each 3–4 cm (1¼–1½ in) across and carried singly on stems up to 20 cm (8 in) long. The selections include 'Wisley Blue' and 'Froyle Mill', the former a deeper blue and the latter a violet-blue; 'Rolf Fiedler', a paler clear blue; and 'Album', white with a violet-blue line on the outside of each petal. 'Alberto Castillo' is the purest white with larger, glistening flowers. Argentina, Uruguay.

Iris

This very large and popular group of plants ranges from the tiny early spring Reticulatas to the huge colourful bearded iris cultivars of late spring and the Japanese water irises of high summer; there is, in short, an iris for almost every purpose. It is a genus of some 250 wild species and a huge number of selections and hybrids, but most of these are rhizomatous and have very different cultivation requirements from the bulbous types that concern us here. Within these there are three groups to consider, the Xiphiums, the Reticulatas and the Junos, and I will deal with them separately, since they are very different in appearance.

In a raised bed in the author's garden, white *Ipheion uniflorum* combines in a charming mid-spring display with dwarf tulips and prostrate spurges.

Xiphium irises

This fairly small group from the western Mediterranean region is quite well known to gardeners and flower arrangers, since it includes the English, Spanish and Dutch irises that are frequently seen as cut flowers. Some of them, particularly the Dutch types, which are a race of vigorous hybrids, make extremely good garden plants and are available in a wide range of colours, so that varieties can be chosen for planting in association with particular schemes. The so-called English iris, *I. latifolia*, is a very easily cultivated border plant. All of them flower rather later on, at the end of the main spring bulb period, into early summer, but nevertheless they are best thought of as spring bulbs, since they die down for the summer and their bulbs need to be slightly drier at this time. Like other spring bulbs, they are obtained and planted in the autumn. An open sunny situation is suitable for *I. xiphium* and the Dutch cultivars, in a soil that is reasonably free-draining, but *I. latifolia* prefers slightly damper conditions. The Xiphium irises have fairly large bulbs with papery brown coats, channelled leaves that are produced mostly near the base of the stem and are often silvery on the upper surface, and flower stems up to 60 cm (2 ft) in height.

Associations: With the great choice of flower colours, there are endless possibilities for planting schemes and, since they are relatively cheap to obtain, it is good fun to experiment. I have had success with both the stronger blues and the white forms of Dutch iris planted in front of a grey-leaved

Abies conifer with the quaking grass *Briza maxima*; and with a clump of yellow irises with Bowles' golden grass, *Milium effusum* 'Aureum', and a backdrop of variegated ivy.

I. × hollandica

This name covers the Dutch iris hybrids that are the best known in the group, mainly as cut flowers. For this purpose they are often forced for winter but, in the garden, they will flower in late spring or early summer. The following are all good varieties, usually 40–60 cm (16 in–2 ft) in height:
'Blue Magic' – violet blue
'Bronze Queen' – bicoloured amber-yellow and bronze
'Golden Harvest' – golden yellow
'Symphony' – bicoloured white and yellow
'White Excelsior' – white, striped yellow on each outer petal

I. latifolia

This was mistakenly thought to be British, hence the name English iris. It is a good garden plant, preferring slightly damper conditions than the other Xiphiums. The stout stems, 45–75 cm (18 in–2½ ft) tall, carry large violet-blue flowers with a yellow mark in the centre of each outer petal. There are named selections with variously coloured flowers, but more often mixed collections are offered, in varying shades of lavender-blue, deep violet or white. Pyrenees.

I. xiphium

The Spanish iris is more slender than the others, usually 30–45 cm (12–18 in) in height with narrow leaves and flowering in mid to late spring. The flowers may be blue, violet, yellow, white, bronze or bicoloured and are slightly smaller than those of the Dutch or English irises, with narrower petals. As with the English iris, there are named cultivars but it is more usual to find mixed colours. Spain, Portugal, North Africa.

The Xiphium group of irises are tall, stately plants available in a wide range of colours and useful for placing in small groups amid other perennials.

Reticulata irises

These, the smallest of the bulbous irises, are very early flowering and delightful hardy bulbs for the front of sunny borders or rock gardens, where they can be left undisturbed for as long as they are thriving. They are only 5–10 cm (2–4 in) high at flowering time with, in most cases, one or two narrow, grey-green quadrangular leaves. Their small bulbs, which are covered with netted (reticulate) coats, need to dry out in the summer while dormant, otherwise they may rot. So in areas where this cannot be guaranteed it is best to lift the bulbs after they have died down, or to provide a raised bed of gritty, sharply drained soil that will dry out. I have adopted the latter technique and find it very successful. The bulbs are available from late summer onwards for autumn planting. In areas where they are not easily cultivated outdoors, they are excellent in pots in an unheated glasshouse or frame, providing much interest and enjoyment in the early spring.

Associations: These small irises are best grown with compact alpines or carpeting plants if the elegant iris shape is to be shown off. I love to see them planted among dwarf ornamental grasses such as the small festucas and stipas, and the dry soil conditions in summer created by the grasses seem to suit them. They will also push up through creeping rock plants like

Antennaria dioica, *Paronychia* and the less vigorous alpine phlox varieties.

I. danfordiae

One of the two yellow Reticulata irises, this one has deep-yellow flowers with green spots in the centre and the three inner petals are represented only by tiny bristles. It has the reputation of splitting into many non-flowering bulbs after flowering, and this is justified. I can recommend trying deep planting, about 10 cm (4 in), and feeding it during the growing season with sulphate of potash. Turkey.

I. histrio and its var. aintabensis

Attractive very early-flowering pale blue irises with darker blue blotches and a yellow splash in the centre of three larger petals. They need very good drainage and a hot dry summer, if outdoors, but are easily grown in pots, given slight protection from the elements. Turkey, Lebanon.

I. histrioides

A very hardy species and a good garden plant, flowering almost before the leaves appear and often in late winter. The frost-resistant flowers have wide petals, giving them a substantial appearance, and are mid blue with many prominent dark blotches on the falls. There are some named selections such as 'Major', a large deep-blue form, and 'Lady Beatrix Stanley', paler blue with more conspicuous spotting on the falls. 'George' is a robust hybrid with larger, rich purple flowers. *I. histrioides* is from Turkey.

I. reticulata

This very popular spring bulb is the easiest of the group to grow, forming large clumps when it is growing well. It is highly variable in colour and has been further selected and hybridized in cultivation to give a great choice of named cultivars. The form sold as *I. reticulata* has fragrant dark violet flowers with an orange splash in the centre of each large petal. Middle East.

Other good varieties and hybrids include:
'Cantab' – pale blue with a yellow line on each outer petal
'Harmony' – rich blue with a yellow line
'J. S. Dijt' – reddish-purple with a yellow line
'Natascha' – very pale icy-blue with a yellow line
'Pauline' – purple with a white, dark-blotched patch in the centre
'Spring Time' – blue with violet tips and a central white patch

I. winogradowii

A lovely plant with large, primrose-yellow flowers produced before the leaves. It grows best in cooler, slightly moister climates, for example in Scottish gardens, where I have seen large patches. 'Katharine Hodgkin', a hybrid between *I. winogradowii* and the blue *I. histrioides*, has a curious mix of colours, a yellowish ground colour with blue veining and spotting, and is very vigorous, soon increasing into clumps. Other named hybrids with the same parentage are 'Frank Elder' and 'Sheila Ann Germany', both slightly bluer in appearance. *I. winogradowii* is from the Caucasus.

Juno irises

This is a large and fascinating group, but few are in general cultivation and most are quite tricky to grow, plants to be cosseted in pots under glass. There are, however, a few that are excellent in the garden. The Junos (subgenus Scorpiris) are distinctive in that their bulbs have fleshy roots, sometimes thick and radish-like, and channelled leaves that make them look like small leek plants; the flowers appear in the leaf axils and are also characteristic in that their three inner petals are small and project horizontally or downwards at the base of the flower. The species recommended below may be planted outside in an open, sunny, well-drained situation during the autumn.

Associations: Since they require warm sunny situations, I have found that the taller Juno irises associate well with small

sun-loving shrubs such as lavender, rosemary and cistus, which give the leafy stems some support and protection from stormy mid-spring weather and use up excess moisture in summer.

I. aucheri

A stocky plant, 15–30 cm (6–12 in) at flowering time with three to six variable flowers from pale blue-lavender to deep violet or white. Turkey, Iran, Iraq, Syria.

I. bucharica

A very easy Juno iris 20–40 cm (8–16 in) tall with glossy green leaves and three to six flowers, either bicoloured white with yellow falls or wholly yellow, usually with greenish markings in the centre of the falls. Central Asia.

I. cyclogossa

Although rare in cultivation, this is worth mentioning since it is superb and easy to cultivate in an open sunny spot. It grows up to 50 cm (20 in) tall with narrow leaves and wiry stems, so has a slender appearance, but the flowers are large, 8–10 cm (3⅛–4 in) across, clove-scented and a lovely clear blue-violet with a yellow blotch in the centre of each outer petal. Afghanistan.

I. graeberiana

This has leafy stems to 35 cm (14 in) in height with four to six pale lavender-blue flowers, with a white or pale yellow crest in the centre of each of the falls. Central Asia.

I. magnifica

As its name suggests, this is one of the best, up to 60 cm (2 ft) tall with scattered, elegantly arched leaves all the way up the stem. The three to seven flowers are soft lavender and about 7–8 cm (2¾–3⅛ in) across, large for a Juno iris; they have a bright yellow zone in the centre of each of the falls, a marking retained in the attractive white form, 'Alba'. Central Asia.

Top: The curiously coloured *Iris* 'Katharine Hodgkin' among later-flowering alpines.

Bottom: Few of the Juno irises will grow outdoors, but *I. cycloglossa* does well.

Right: The spring and summer snowflakes both like damp soils. Here, *Leucojum aestivum* grows with fritillaries by a garden pond.

Opposite: Most grape hyacinths are blue but this is the white form of the tassel hyacinth, *Muscari comosum*.

Ixiolirion

Although not cultivated to any great extent, this bulb is inexpensive and quite showy when growing well, having slender stems and elegant funnel-shaped blue flowers in late spring, and looking rather like a small trumpet lily. The bulbs are planted in autumn in a warm sunny situation where they will dry out in summer after flowering; they seem to do best in alkaline soils.

Associations: These are good companions for other plants with similar sun-loving requirements, such as the winter-flowering *Iris unguicularis*. The strong blue colour also goes well with the blue-grey foliage of euphorbias.

I. tataricum
The branched flower stems about 30–35 cm (12–14 in) in height are accompanied by long narrow leaves and carry several bright blue funnel-shaped flowers 3–5 cm (1¼–2 in) long in late spring. Turkey to central Asia.

Leucojum

The charming snowflakes are close relatives of the better-known snowdrops, but have flowers with six equal petals, rather than three large outer and three small inner petals. The spring snowflake, *L. vernum*, often flowers so early as almost to qualify for the winter section, followed much later by the summer snowflake, *L. aestivum*. These two are very easily cultivated in a damp situation in heavy soil, in full sun or partial shade, and can soon form good-sized clumps. The much smaller *L. nicaeense* is really better in pots or in a rock garden, where it can be seen more closely. Leucojums should be planted in early autumn, or soon after flowering while the leaves are still green.

Associations: The spring and summer snowflakes are excellent in damp grassland, their natural habitat, and are especially effective when grown alongside a stream or pool. *L. vernum* will grow well under deciduous shrubs and is useful for naturalizing in such situations, for example with the coloured twigs of coppiced willows, *Salix alba* var. *vitellina* and 'Britzensis', or with winter-flowering *Viburnum farreri* and *V.* × *bodnantense*.

L. aestivum
The tallest species, with strap-shaped bright green leaves and a 30–45 cm (12–18 in) stem carrying up to five pendent bells, 3–4 cm (1¼–1½ in) across, which are white

with green tips. 'Gravetye Giant' is a vigorous, large-flowered form which can reach 90 cm (3 ft) in height when given moist growing conditions. Europe, Turkey.

L. nicaeense

A tiny, delicate species only 10 cm (4 in) or less in height with narrow dark green leaves and one or two small pure white bells. Southern France.

L. vernum

An excellent garden plant, robust and flowering very early, but stocky and standing up well to the weather. At first it is only 5–10 cm (2–4 in) in height, but it elongates during flowering to about 20 cm (8 in), accompanied by strap-like glossy green leaves. The normal form has one large bell per stem, with green tips to the petals, but var. *carpathicum* has yellow tips, and var. *vagneri* is robust, with two flowers per stem. Europe.

Muscari

The reputation of the grape hyacinths has suffered because of the tendency to weediness of the very common *M. neglectum*, but there are some very splendid garden plants within this small genus, suitable for sunny or partially shaded positions at the front of borders or in rock gardens. Most of the species have dense spikes of small blue egg-shaped, oblong or nearly spherical flowers with the mouth crimped in, but a few are bell-like, and some are not blue. The bulbs are obtainable in autumn and should be planted soon afterwards, since their roots

start into growth quickly, and some also produce leaves in the autumn.

Associations: The more vigorous species, such as *M. neglectum* and *M. armeniacum*, are best for naturalizing beneath deciduous shrubs, and, since they flower in mid to late spring, are ideal for associating with early shrubs like forsythia and magnolias; a blue haze of grape hyacinths beneath either of these is a simple but delightful combination. I have a self-seeding patch of the striking *M. latifolium* with a backdrop of a dwarf grey-leaved *Abies* conifer, which is also very effective.

M. armeniacum

A very free-flowering and easily cultivated species with narrow basal leaves and dense 15–20 cm (6–8 in) racemes of mid violet-blue flowers. There is a 'double' version,

'Blue Spike', with large solid spikes of flowers, which is suitable for bedding schemes because of its mass effect, but individually it lacks the grace of the normal form. Turkey, Caucasus.

M. aucheri

One of the smaller species, this is a 'refined' plant with two grey-green leaves and an 8–12 cm (3⅛–4¾ in) raceme of bright clear blue flowers, with a 'topknot' of pale or almost white sterile flowers. Turkey.

M. azureum (Hyacinthus azureus)

As its name suggests, this is bright sky-blue. The two or three grey-green leaves are short at flowering time, accompanying 5–12 cm (2–4¾ in) tall, densely flowered racemes of small bell-shaped flowers, not closed in at the mouth. Turkey.

M. botryoides

This has dense racemes up to 15 cm (6 in) in height carrying many small, nearly spherical brilliant blue flowers. It prefers cooler, moist positions and looks good near a pond. There is an attractive white form, 'Album'. Central and south-east Europe.

M. comosum

A rather different-looking species, since the racemes are crowned by a tuft of brightly coloured sterile flowers, hence the common name 'tassel hyacinth'. It is taller, at 30–60 cm (1–2 ft), with oblong-tubular brownish flowers loosely spaced up the stem; the tassel flowers at the top are bright violet, carried on long violet stalks. There is an albino form with a white tassel, 'Album'. Mediterranean region to Iran.

Right: *Narcissus cyclamineus* requires a damp soil. It is the parent of a whole range of attractive hybrids.

Opposite top: A cool combination of *Narcissus* 'Ice Follies' and *Helleborus foetidus* in the Bagatelle Garden, Paris.
Bottom: One of the Cyclamineus hybrids, *Narcissus* 'Dove Wings' with *Erica carnea* and the caper spurge, *Euphorbia lathyris.*

M. latifolium

A handsome grape hyacinth with one broad, grey-green leaf and a 15–30 cm (6–12 in) raceme of oblong blackish-violet flowers, topped with a cluster of paler blue sterile ones. Turkey.

M. muscarimi (M. moschatum)

The musk hyacinth is not as easy to cultivate as the grape hyacinths, requiring a hot sunny position to ripen the bulbs and encourage them to flower. It is about 10–15 cm (4–6 in) in height with short dense racemes of tubular flowers, smoky white with a musk-like scent. Sometimes available is *M. ambrosiacum* with pale, translucent blue flowers. *M. macrocarpum* is perhaps the best of this trio but has longer (about 1 cm/½ in) dull violet flowers, changing to bright yellow and having a very strong fruity aroma. Turkey, Aegean islands.

Narcissus

For those in temperate climates, daffodils are the real heralds of spring, especially the large yellow trumpet types and the hundreds of wonderful hybrids now available to us. These will be mentioned below, but first let us look at some of the wild species from which they have been derived over a long and skilful process of plant breeding. Daffodils are so familiar that they scarcely need a description, with their central 'corona' surrounded by six petals, but within this basic shape there is a great range of form, from the small-cupped poet's narcissus and the tazettas through to the deeper-cupped and long trumpet types; sometimes the petals are held out flat, sometimes sharply reflexed as in *N. cyclamineus*; and the number of flowers per stem ranges from one to several in an umbel, as in the tazetta group. On the whole, daffodils are relatively easy to grow in any reasonably well-drained soil that does not get too dry in summer, although some of the smaller species, such as *N. watieri*, do need a warm, dryish dormant period if they are to flower well the following season, as do the Mediterranean *N. papyraceus* and *N. tazetta*. Daffodils are best planted in early autumn, since they start to root early. If they are doing well and flowering freely, it is best to leave them undisturbed to grow into clumps, but if flowering becomes sparse it is worth lifting and dividing the clumps or feeding them with a potash-rich fertilizer in spring and autumn. After flowering, the leaves should be left as long as possible, since they are essential if the bulbs are to maintain their vigour; experiments have indicated that the leaves must be left untouched for at least six weeks after flowering, and preferably longer.

Associations: Daffodils in grass are one of the delights of spring and it is difficult to surpass this for effect. However, using them in clumps in perennial borders and between shrubs allows for a great deal of experimental fun. I once saw a drift of the primrose-and-white 'Ice Follies' in the Bagatelle Garden in Paris planted with *Helleborus foetidus*, two common plants combined in a delightful cool spring display. In my own garden, a favourite planting is the Cyclamineus hybrid 'Dove Wings' with winter heathers, which are just reaching the end of their flowering period as 'Dove Wings' reaches its peak.

N. alpestris

I mention this since it is a particular favourite, but it is not at all common in nurseries or gardens. It is a small trumpet daffodil 15–25 cm (6–10 in) tall with pendent creamy-white flowers, very like the long-cultivated *N. moschatus*, although that too is rare nowadays. Pyrenees.

N. assoanus

This small jonquil narcissus may be referred to as '*N. juncifolius*' or '*N. requienii*'. It is 10–20 cm (4–8 in) in height with nearly cylindrical green leaves and the stems carry one or two fragrant small-cupped yellow flowers 1.5–2.5 cm (⅝–1 in) across. Spain, south-west France.

N. asturiensis (N. minimus)

A tiny, delightful and easily cultivated trumpet daffodil with narrow grey-green leaves and a 5–10 cm (2–4 in) stem bearing one rich yellow flower 1–1.5 cm (½–⅝ in) long; the trumpet has an attractively frilled rim. *N. minor* is very similar but slightly

larger in all its parts, 15–25 (6–10 in) tall with wider leaves and larger deep-yellow flowers. Spain, Portugal, France.

N. bulbocodium

Some forms of this narcissus flower so early that I have included details of it on page 114, together with its relatives *N. cantabricus* and *N. romieuxii*.

N. cyclamineus

This must be regarded as among the best of all the small narcissus species and very easy to cultivate in a damp, cool site. It is about 10–20 cm (4–8 in) in height with narrow

bright green leaves and very distinctive rich yellow flowers, which have their petals sharply reflexed, leaving the 1.5–2 cm (⅝–¾ in) long trumpet thrusting forward. It grows very well in damp grassland, provided that the grasses forming the turf are not very coarse. Portugal, Spain.

N. jonquilla

The jonquil is a popular cut flower in the winter months and is especially welcome because of its strong perfume. The wild form is 25–30 cm (10–12 in) in height with long dark-green, rush-like leaves and an umbel of two to five deep-yellow flowers which are 2–3.5 cm (¾–1⅜ in) in diameter and have a long slender tube. Portugal, Spain.

N. papyraceus

The paper-white narcissus is best known as a plant for rapid forcing for a winter display, but it does grow well in the garden in sheltered sunny positions protected from the worst of the frosts. I have a flourishing clump flowering freely every year on the sunny side of a glasshouse. It has broad strap-shaped, grey-green leaves and umbels of up to twenty glistening white fragrant small-cupped flowers, each 2.5–4 cm (1–1½ in) across. Bulbs forced for the winter will flower in six weeks without the initial cool growing period that hyacinths need. Western Mediterranean.

N. poeticus

The poet's narcissus or pheasant's eye is one of the last of all to flower, in late spring. It is excellent for growing in damp grassland, its natural habitat, and extends the flowering season in grassy areas that have been set aside for spring bulbs. It is fairly tall, at 30–45 cm (12–18 in), each stem carrying a solitary flat, white, intensely fragrant flower 4–5 cm (1½–2 in) in diameter, which has a very shallow, frilled, greenish-yellow cup with a red or orange rim. Southern Europe.

N. pseudonarcissus

The wild trumpet daffodil or Lent lily has, through a long process of hybridization and selection, given us many large-flowered cultivars. The wild forms are fairly short, stocky plants with one flower per stem, pale yellow with a darker yellow trumpet that is expanded and frilled at the mouth, whereas the Tenby daffodil, subsp. *obvallaris*, has smallish, wholly deep-yellow flowers. Both are very easy to cultivate and are valuable for naturalizing in grass or deciduous woodland. Western Europe.

N. rupicola

A delightful miniature, 10–15 cm (4–6 in) in height with narrow grey-green leaves and small deep-yellow fragrant flowers 1.5–3 cm (⅝–1¼ in) in diameter with a shallow six-lobed cup in the centre. Although excellent for an unheated glasshouse, where it can be appreciated more fully, it will grow well in a sharply drained sunny spot. Spain, Portugal.

N. tazetta

The cluster-headed, highly perfumed Tazetta narcissus has been popular for centuries. It varies considerably, from

Drifts of Narcissus pseudonarcissus growing in damp grassland.

15 to 50 cm (6–20 in) in height, flowering between late autumn and spring, and bicoloured white with a yellow cup, yellow with an orange cup, or yellow throughout. Each stem carries an umbel of up to twenty flowers, which are 2.5–4 cm (1–1½ in) in diameter with a small cup 5–10 mm (¼–½ in) across. The best-known garden representative is 'Soleil d'Or', a popular cut flower in the winter months. *N. tazetta* is rather tender and, in cold areas, requires a sheltered sunny position if it is to survive the winter undamaged; the dormant bulbs also need a warm rest period in summer to initiate flower buds. *N. canaliculatus* is very similar, but smaller and more slender with creamy, orange-cupped flowers. Mediterranean region.

N. triandrus

The angel's tears daffodil is a graceful little plant with narrow dark green leaves and stems 10–20 cm (4–8 in) tall carrying one to six pendent creamy-white or soft yellow flowers, which have a deep cup 1–1.5 cm (½–⅝ in) long and six reflexed petals. The creamy 'Albus' is the form most frequently cultivated, a charming plant for dappled shade or a cool spot in a rock garden. Portugal, Spain.

N. watieri

A beautiful, rather rare species, which is best grown in pots in an unheated glasshouse, since its bulbs need to be warm and fairly dry in summer if they are to flower well. It is 10–12 cm (4–4¾ in) in height with narrow grey-green leaves and solitary flattish white, small-cupped flowers, 2–2.5 cm (¾–1 in) in diameter. North Africa.

Narcissus hybrids

The countless narcissus hybrids have been classified into groups by Britain's Royal Horticultural Society and I have chosen a few examples from each of these groups, or Divisions, as they are known:

1. Trumpet daffodils

One flower per stem; trumpet as long as, or longer than, the petals.
'Bravoure' – bicoloured, pure white petals with yellow trumpet
'Dutch Master' – deep golden yellow throughout
'Empress of Ireland' – a beautiful clean white throughout

2. Large-cupped daffodils

One flower per stem; cup more than one-third the length of, but less than equal to, the petals.
'Carlton' – sulphur-yellow petals and yellow cup

'Professor Einstein' – white petals with striking orange-red cup
'St Patrick's Day' – lemon-yellow petals with pale lemon cup

3. Small-cupped daffodils

One flower per stem; cup not more than one-third the length of the petals.
'Birma' – sulphur-yellow petals with a small orange cup
'Dallas' – white petals and white cup with a green centre
'Sabine Hay' – orange petals with a red cup

4. Double daffodils

One or more flowers per stem; with doubling of the petals or cup, or both.
'Irene Copeland' – long segments cream, short ones yellow-apricot
'Rip van Winkle' – only 10–12 cm (4–4¾ in), many narrow yellow segments
'Tahiti' – petals golden with the double centre orange and yellow

5. Triandrus daffodils

Characteristics of *N. triandrus* clearly evident; usally two or more flowers per stem; petals reflexed.
'Hawera' – 20–25 cm (8–10 in) tall with up to six small lemon-yellow flowers
'Liberty Bells' – tall, with one to three large nodding lemon flowers
'Tresamble' – nodding, wholly clean white flowers

6. Cyclamineus daffodils

Characteristics of *N. cyclamineus* clearly evident; usally one flower per stem; petals reflexed.

'Dove Wings' – reflexed white petals and a pale yellow cup.
'February Gold' – wholly golden yellow
'Foundling' – petals white, cup deep rose
'Jetfire' – golden-yellow petals, bright orange trumpet

7. Jonquilla daffodils

Characteristics of *N. jonquilla* clearly evident; usually one to three fragrant flowers on a rounded stem; leaves narrow, dark green; petals spreading, not reflexed.
'Lintie' – petals yellow, cup deep orange
'Pipit' – petals lemon, white at base, cup lemon and white
'Sweetness' – rich golden yellow throughout, 35–40 cm (14–16 in) in height

8. Tazetta daffodils

Characteristics of *N. tazetta* clearly evident; usually between three and twenty fragrant flowers per stem; leaves broad; petals spreading, not reflexed.
'Geranium' – creamy-white petals, rich orange cup
'Minnow' – small, at 20 cm (8 in) tall; lemon petals, deeper-yellow cup
'Scarlet Gem' – buff-yellow petals, frilly orange cup

9. Poeticus daffodils

Characteristics of *N. poeticus* without admixture of any other; usually one fragrant flower per stem; petals pure white; cup disc-shaped with a green or yellow centre and a red rim.
'Cantabile' – petals white, cup green with a narrow red rim

10. Species, wild variants and wild hybrids

A selection of these has been described above.

11. Split-corona ('Collar' or 'orchid-flowered') daffodils

Cup split rather than lobed, and usually for more than half its length.
'Cassata' – petals white, split segments of cup yellow
'Tricolet' – petals white, cup split into three amber segments

Nectaroscordum

This onion relative is unusual, not showy but with attractive pendent bells that are like small fritillaries, several in an umbel on long arching stalks. In the fruiting stage these turn upwards to make a shuttlecock-like arrangement and are good for drying. It is easily cultivated in almost any soil in sun or dappled shade and will seed itself around, sometimes too readily. The bad thing about this plant is its smell – quite the most pungent, clinging onion-like smell I have encountered, but it only emits this if it is damaged, so you have been warned! The bulbs should be planted in autumn.

A late-flowering Jonquil hybrid, *Narcissus* 'Baby Moon', growing with Bowles' golden grass and hostas.

Associations: With its subdued flower colours and interestingly shaped flower heads, this bulb really needs to be planted where it will stand above other plants, and preferably against a dark background. A clump sited in front of dark evergreens shows up quite well.

N. siculum (N. dioscoridis)

Long, narrow, sharply keeled leaves accompany tall wiry stems to 1.5 m (5 ft) in height in late spring, each with a large, loosely flowered umbel of up to thirty bell-shaped pendent whitish flowers, suffused maroon and stained green towards the base; they are about 1.5–2.5 cm (⅝–1 in) long. Southern France, Italy.

Ornithogalum

These comprise a sizeable group of plants in Europe, Asia and Africa which are not rated very highly as garden subjects, although they are easily cultivated and can provide considerable interest in spring. They will grow in sun or semi-shade, but must receive some sun or their flowers will not open to reveal the startlingly white interior. Most of the hardy species have upward-facing starry white flowers, hence their common name of Star of Bethlehem. They can be grown in ordinary, reasonably well-drained soil, planted in autumn following their summer dormancy.

Cistus purpureus provides a natural associate for the Mediterranean Ornithogalum narbonense.

Associations: The common *O. umbellatum* is very suitable for naturalizing in situations where it will receive at least dappled sunlight, and associates very well with blue forget-me-nots, which flower at about the same time. *O. nutans* will take rather more shade and is excellent in grass or beneath deciduous shrubs.

O. arabicum

A tall, rather tender species, requiring a sheltered sunny situation, where the bulbs will receive a warm dry summer rest. The broad, grey-green overwintering leaves are produced in a basal tuft, then in late spring it produces a 50–75 cm (20 in–2½ ft) stem carrying a flat-topped head of large creamy-white, black-eyed flowers. Mediterranean region.

O. balansae

One of the shortest, earliest-flowering species, with two glossy green leaves and 5–10 cm (2–4 in) stems bearing up to five erect white flowers. Its size makes it very suitable for a rock garden or raised bed. Turkey.

O. nutans

An unusual late-spring species with 15–25 cm (6–10 in) racemes of pendent silvery-white flowers, which are soft green on the outside and have elegantly recurved petals. It does well in partial shade. Europe.

O. sibthorpii

This is a very compact species with narrow basal leaves and near-stemless heads of flowers nestling among them, white inside and green on the outside. It is excellent for a sunny situation and soon forms large clumps. *O. tenuifolium* is similar but usually slightly taller. Both Mediterranean region.

O. umbellatum

Perhaps one of the commonest in cultivation, ideal for naturalizing in grass or in partially sunny positions beneath and between shrubs. It has narrow dark-green, white-striped leaves and large upright flowers carried in a loose raceme, shiny white inside, green on the outside. Europe.

Puschkinia

This is very similar in overall appearance to the scillas, but the flowers have a short tube and a small cup in the centre. It requires a cool position where the bulbs will not become hot and dry when they are dormant in summer. A humus-rich soil in dappled shade is suitable and, after planting in autumn, they are best left undisturbed for as long as they are doing well.

Associations: With their liking for cool growing conditions, try puschkinias among dwarf rhododendrons and other 'peat garden' plants; they will bring interest to the area before these have started their display.

P. scilloides

The Lebanon squill is only 5–10 cm (2–4 in) in height with two basal leaves and short spikes of pale blue flowers 1–1.5 cm (½–⅝ in) across, which have a darker blue stripe along the centre of each petal; there is also a white form, 'Alba'. Middle East.

Romulea

The Mediterranean species of the crocus-like romuleas are quite pleasing little bulbs for a warm sunny situation, but many of those from southern Africa have much larger, showier flowers in a great range of colours. Most of the latter are not hardy but can be grown in a frost-free glasshouse or conservatory. The small corms are planted in the autumn and dried off in summer when they have died down. Most seem to do best in a rather sandy soil mix.

Associations: In order for the flowers to open out properly, romuleas need to be planted where they will receive plenty of sun in spring, so an open spot where they will not be shaded by other plants is best, although I have had some success growing them through dwarf carpeting plants such as the creeping silvery *Paronychia* species, which provide some protection during frosty periods.

R. bulbocodium

The best-known of the hardier species with slender wiry leaves and upright funnel-shaped lilac-blue flowers which open to about 3 cm across. *R. nivalis* is similar in overall appearance but has more colourful flowers, often a stronger bluish-lilac with a deep-yellow throat. Mediterranean region.

Scilla

Scillas, collectively known as the squills, are mostly dwarf spring bulbs with short racemes of blue flowers, but there are a few that deviate from this and flower in late spring or summer, and a few even flower in autumn. The early ones are the most valuable, since they provide one of the first splashes of colour of the season and are not too fastidious about their conditions. Some of the showiest are most suited to dappled shade, where they will not become too hot and dry in summer. In view of their size, they are ideal for growing at the front of borders with perennials such as hellebores and hostas and, in quantity, can be naturalized under deciduous trees and shrubs. A few of the Mediterranean species, such as *S. peruviana* and *S. litardierei*, require a warm sunny situation. Scilla bulbs are obtained and planted in autumn in a reasonably well-drained soil.

Associations: *S. bifolia*, *S. bithynica*, *S. lilio-hyacinthus*, *S. mischtschenkoana* 'Tubergeniana' and *S. sibirica* associate well with perennials and shrubs in dappled shade, provided that the area is not regularly and intensively cultivated, since they are best left undisturbed. In these areas they are extremely useful for lengthening the season of interest and for enhancing plantings of early perennials such as hellebores and pulmonarias. They can also be planted beneath early deciduous magnolias, forsythias and viburnums with great effect.

S. bifolia

A very easily cultivated early-flowering scilla, 5–10 cm (2–4 in) tall with two basal leaves and short racemes of small starry, deep-violet flowers. There are named forms such as 'Alba' (white), 'Rosea' (pink) and 'Praecox', a very vigorous early form. Europe, Turkey.

The Siberian squill *Scilla sibirica* will naturalize under shrubs but is equally valuable for an early spring display in containers. It is seen here growing under a bay tree with *Daphne mezereum*.

S. bithynica

An excellent mid-spring scilla with narrowly strap-shaped leaves and racemes of small bright mid-blue flattish flowers up to 15 cm (6 in) in height; it is useful for naturalizing, setting large amounts of seed. *S. italica* is similar in appearance but has tapered leaves and more cone-shaped racemes. *S. bithynica* is from Turkey and *S. italica* from Western Europe.

S. lilio-hyacinthus

An unusual squill with lily-like scaly bulbs and a tuft of broad glossy green leaves. The small lilac-blue or white ('Alba') flowers appear in late spring, carried in a raceme 15–25 cm (6–10 in) tall. Western Europe.

S. litardierei

One of the later-flowering species for a sunny position, this is also known as *S. pratensis*. It has several narrow leaves and dense 10–20 cm (4–8 in) racemes of many small bright blue flowers. Dalmatia.

S. mischtschenkoana 'Tubergeniana'

One of the best of the early-spring squills, only 5–12 cm (2–4¾ in) tall with a few large flowers on each stem, which are pale blue with a darker blue stripe on each petal, bell-shaped at first, opening out nearly flat in the sun. Iran.

S. peruviana

A robust species with a rosette of many sword-shaped leaves appearing in autumn, accompanied in late spring by large, 15–25 cm (6–10 in) high, densely flowered conical heads of steely-blue flowers, white in the form 'Alba'. It needs a warm sunny position. Mediterranean region.

S. sibirica

This is the well-known very early-flowering Siberian squill, much loved for its intensely blue nodding bells – only a few on each 5–10 cm (2–4 in) stem. 'Spring Beauty' is a very rich colour but all forms are good, including 'Alba', the white form. Western Asia.

Tecophilaea

The cost of the amazing Chilean blue crocus usually dictates that it will be cosseted in a pot in an unheated glasshouse, but I have found that it does quite well outside in an open sunny bed of gritty/sandy soil and has survived periods when the soil was frozen solid. However, this is such a dramatic plant that there is a lot to be said for growing it inside, where its flowers can really be appreciated. When available, the corms are offered in the autumn catalogues.

Associations: Although it is unlikely that many gardeners will have the opportunity to try companion plantings of *Tecophilaea*, I think that, if asked, I would recommend placing it alongside something neutral and greyish, which would complement rather than compete with the intense blue.

T. cyanocrocus

When in flower the plant is 5–10 cm (2–4 in) in height with narrow green leaves and vivid dark blue, widely funnel-shaped flowers 3 cm (1¼ in) across. There is a paler-blue selection with a white eye, var. *leichtlinii*, and a purplish one, var. *violacea*. Chilean Andes.

Trillium

North America has given us the best species in this lovely genus, beautiful woodlanders that have three leaves in a whorl and flowers that have three narrow sepals and three enlarged, showier petals. These are plants that need plenty of moisture throughout their spring growing season, and they will grow happily in quite damp situations with a good humus content. The rhizomes should never be dried out, so it is best to obtain them as growing plants in pots and, having planted them, they are best left to build up slowly into clumps. Situations in dappled shade suit them well, although in cooler climates they will take almost full sun if there is plenty of moisture at their roots. Planting can take place at any time, although late summer is a good time, allowing them to become established before the drier summer months.

Associations: To my mind, trilliums look best when there is little around to compete with them, except perhaps for dead leaves, pine needles or bark chips as a background to their subtly beautiful form. If other plants are nearby, they need to be of quite different appearance so that the trilliums stand out. A natural combination that I once saw on Mount Hood in Oregon combined the delicate ferny leaves of *Dicentra formosa* with *T. ovatum*; this worked beautifully, but I have not yet tried it in the garden.

T. cernuum

This is one of the most modest of plants, 25–40 cm (10–16 in) in height, with white

For cool, shady positions, the beautiful trilliums have few equals. This is a white form of the Californian *T. chloropetalum*.

or pink-flushed flowers hanging down below the whorl of three unmottled leaves, thus hidden from above and requiring an attitude of prayer to view it! A position on top of a bank would be ideal for it. *T. vaseyi* is similar but the flowers are much larger and showier, with petals 4.5–5.5 cm (1¾–2¼ in) long in deep maroon. Both eastern North America.

T. chloropetalum

There are several similar-looking species in cultivation, the naming of which has been, and still is, much confused. These are the 'sessile' trilliums, in which each stem bears a whorl of three beautifully mottled leaves upon which sits a stemless upright funnel-shaped flower. The flowers are up to 10 cm (4 in) long and may be white, yellow-green or deep reddish-purple. *T. cuneatum* is very

like this, certainly in garden value, and so is *T. sessile*, although the latter has much smaller flowers at about 2–4.5 cm (¾–1¾ in) long. *T. luteum* is similar in form, but with cool pale yellow or greenish-yellow flowers. *T. chloropetalum* is Californian, and the other three are from the eastern United States.

T. erectum

A very easily cultivated trillium, 25–45 cm (10–16 in) tall with plain green leaves overtopped by a stalked flower, which can be up to 8 cm (3⅛ in) long and 5 cm (2 in) across, although is often much less. My favourite forms are those with deep maroon petals, but the colour varies a lot and may also be white or yellowish. The flowers have a smell reminiscent of a wet dog! Eastern United States.

T. grandiflorum

The wake robin is generally acknowledged to be the finest trillium, with a stout stem up to 45 cm (18 in) in height carrying a whorl of broad plain green leaves and a large glistening white flower with petals 5–9 cm (2–3½ in) long; as the flowers mature they become pinkish, but there is a rare type, 'Roseum', which is soft pink all the time. A double version, with many more petals than normal, is known as 'Flore Pleno'. Eastern North America. Its western North American relative, *T. ovatum*, is very similar but is often slightly smaller and the flowers are usually more widely open.

T. nivale

One of the smaller species at only 5–8 cm (2–3⅛ in) in height, but just as lovely as any of the larger ones. The unmottled dark green leaves act as a perfect foil for the snowy-white flowers, which may be up to 4.5 cm (1¾ in) long. This is one trillium that appears to like limestone in the soil and, having learned that fact some years ago, I now have a flourishing clump. Eastern United States.

T. rivale

If anything, this is smaller than *T. nivale*, only 5 cm (2 in) tall with a whorl of unmottled leaves overtopped by white flowers, which have a variable amount of red spotting inside; some selections have more prominent spotting, as in 'Purple Heart', while others are wholly pink-flushed. It grows well and increases on my 'peat' bed, which consists more of rotting logs and leafmould than actual peat. Oregon, California.

Triteleia

Triteleias, like their relatives the brodiaeas, are among the last of all the spring bulbs to flower and overlap into the domain of the summer perennials, but they die down for the heat of the summer and begin to root again in the autumn, so their corms should be planted by mid autumn. They are very similar in appearance to brodiaeas and are often found in books and catalogues under that name – the main difference being that brodiaeas have three proper stamens and triteleias six. For the purposes of garden value, there is little difference, their stiff flower stems bearing umbels of starry or funnel-shaped flowers, and they are just as easy to grow in an open sunny situation.

Associations: Triteleias are useful in situations where earlier flowering bulbs have finished and there is a late-spring gap before the summer perennials and shrubs take over. I have them growing adjacent to plants such as *Iris unguicularis*, grey-leaved helichrysums and lavender, all of which enjoy warm sunny places.

T. hyacinthina

Although not showy, this is well worth having, with stems up to 45 cm (18 in) tall carrying compact umbels 5–8 cm (2–3⅛ in) across of almost flat and starry white or very pale blue flowers, each 1.5–2.5 cm (⅝–1 in) across. Western United States.

T. ixioides

This has cheerful starry yellow flowers in umbels about 10 cm (4 in) in diameter. Its height is 30–35 cm (12–14 in). California.

T. laxa

Perhaps the showiest species, this is 30–45 cm (12–18 in) in height, with 10–16 cm (4–6¼ in) diameter umbels of large blue funnel-shaped flowers up to 5 cm (2 in) in length, usually rich blue but quite variable in depth of colour. California, Oregon.

T. × tubergenii

This is a hybrid involving *T. laxa* and is very similar, with mid-blue flowers. 'Queen Fabiola' is another of the same type, its flowers a rather deeper blue. All are excellent and there is little to choose between them as garden plants. Garden hybrid.

Tulipa

The mention of tulips immediately calls to mind the great array of large-flowered hybrid cultivars that are such a splendid feature of mid-spring parks and gardens and an essential element of gardening throughout the temperate parts of the world. I would hate to be without a few selected varieties in the garden, for they are ideal for providing a welcome splash of colour in what could otherwise justifiably be referred to as a botanical collection. I tend to prefer the charm of the wild species, which are no less colourful, but

Above: The western American triteleias and brodiaeas flower so late that they overlap with the first of the summer bulbs. Here, *T. x tubergenii* can be seen with *Lilium regale* amid *Helichrysum italicum* and Cistus.

Opposite: *Tulipa clusiana chrysantha* needs an open, well-drained spot where its bulbs will be hot and dry in summer.

there is a place for both the species and their horticultural offspring when they are used in the right setting.

Tulips are not difficult to cultivate and keep from year to year, provided that their basic needs are understood. The main requirement is that the bulbs become dry and relatively warm during their summer rest. Good drainage is thus very important, but soil type appears to be not so critical, for although tulips are often associated with limestones in the wild, alkaline soil does not seem to be essential for success with them in gardens. In areas with damp summers it is better to lift the bulbs and store them dry over the summer months, and with bedding schemes this is more convenient since the space will be required for something else in summer.

All tulips are offered for sale in autumn and should be planted at this time, although a delay until late autumn is not a problem, since they do not start to root very early.

Associations: Many of the tulips have startlingly bright flowers, so it is advantageous to plant them with neutral grey or silvery foliage plants, which really set them off well. The smaller species, for example the brilliant scarlet *T. linifolia* and *T. clusiana*, are very effective in creating arresting splashes of colour amid the ornamental perennial grey grasses, and also with early flowering alpines like the yellow-flowered *Alyssum saxatile* and the compact *Erysimum* varieties 'Jubilee Gem' and 'Wenlock Beauty'. The dwarf yellow *T. batalinii*, *T. tarda* and *T. urumiensis* are perfect companions for the prostrate blue-

grey leaves and yellow-green flower heads of *Euphorbia myrsinites*. The taller, rather quaint *T. acuminata* is much enhanced when planted with grey-leaved sun-loving subjects such as *Convolvulus cneorum*, artemisias and sage. The large hybrid cultivars are often used for bedding displays, of course, with spectacular results, but on a private garden scale I prefer them in small groups of ten or so, planted closely and informally among shrubs and perennials. One of my favourite plantings in our garden is a group of the early salmon-coloured 'Prinses Irene' on the sunnier side of a creamy *Cytisus praecox*, but there is a tulip to suit every purpose so one can have enormous fun experimenting with associations. Perhaps it is hackneyed, but yellow 'West Point' lily-flowered tulips and blue forget-me-nots are to me still one of the best!

T. acuminata

Although bearing a species name, this is an old hybrid resembling one of the very early tulip selections from Istanbul. It is 45–60 cm (18 in–2 ft) tall with elegant flowers having narrow, long-pointed petals in a mixture of red and yellow.

T. aucheriana

A dwarf species only 8–10 cm (3⅛–4 in) tall with lilac-pink, yellow-centred flowers 6–7 cm (2½–2¾ in) across. Iran.

T. batalinii

A beautiful small tulip 5–15 cm (2–6 in) high with narrow, grey-green undulating leaves and rounded lemon-yellow flowers 5–7 cm (2–2¾ in) in diameter. The similar but brilliant scarlet *T. linifolia* is even more showy, and there are intermediates with apricot and bronzy flowers, such as 'Bronze Charm' and 'Apricot Jewel'. Both species need hot sunny places in a rock garden or raised bed. Central Asia.

T. biflora

A small, slender species 8–15 cm (3⅛–6 in) in height with two narrow grey-green leaves and up to three small white flowers about 3–4 cm (1¼–1½ in) across, with deep-yellow centres and suffused greenish or purplish on the outside. *T. polychroma* is sometimes offered and is very similar, as is *T. turkestanica*, although this has up to twelve flowers on each stem, which may be 20–30 cm (8–12 in) tall. Middle East, central Asia.

Left: The Cretan *Tulipa bakeri* and *Convolvulus cneorum* both enjoy warm sunny positions.

Opposite: The curious *Tulipa acuminata* is similar in shape to some of the elegant Istanbul tulips of the Ottoman Turks. Its mixed colours stand out well against silvery artemisias.

T. clusiana

This is one of the most elegant of species with narrow grey-green leaves and white flowers, which open out to a starry shape to reveal a blackish-crimson eye in the centre; the outside is stained bright crimson.
Its even more colourful variety *chrysantha* is similar in habit but the flowers have a yellow ground colour, flushed red outside. Iran, Afghanistan, Kashmir.

T. fosteriana

This large and well-known tulip has given us some excellent hybrids but the wild species is very showy, 20–45 cm (8–18 in) tall with hairy grey leaves and stems, and huge bowl-shaped red flowers 10–15 cm (4–6 in) across when fully open; the blackish eye is outlined in yellow. Central Asia.

T. greigii

Perhaps one does not readily think of tulips as foliage plants, but this is attractive from the moment it unfurls its broad purple-striped leaves. It is a stocky 15–25 cm (6–10 in) plant with deep-red, black-eyed flowers. Central Asia.

T. hageri, T. orphanidea and T. whittallii

These are grouped together since they are very similar. They are 25–30 cm (10–12 in) in height with narrow leaves and one to three flowers per stem, about 4–5 cm (1½–2 in) across when open. The subdued flower colours are rather appealing, in shades of brownish-orange, bronze or dull red suffused with green. Greece, western Turkey.

T. humilis (T. pulchella, T. violacea)

This is an excellent dwarf tulip for the front of a hot sunny border, only 5–15 cm (2–6 in) in height with 5–7 cm (2–2¾ in) diameter flowers in shades of purple, violet and pink, which may be offered under any of the three names given above. There is also a lovely white form, var. *pallida* (or *caerulea-oculata*), which has a deep-blue eye in the centre. Middle East.

T. kaufmanniana

The waterlily tulip is one of the earliest-flowering tulips and varies widely in colour, although the flowers are frequently creamy or primrose with a reddish exterior. The broad grey basal leaves are short at flowering time, and the whole plant is only 10–20 cm (4–8 in) tall but is very sturdy, standing up well to the early spring weather. At first the flowers are goblet-shaped but then open out to 10 cm (4 in) or more across. Central Asia.

T. kolpakowskiana

An attractive small-flowered slender species 10–20 cm (4–8 in) tall with yellow flowers, becoming darker towards the centre and flushed with pink or green on the outside, opening to about 6–8 cm (2½–3⅛ in). Central Asia.

T. marjolettii

Probably not a wild species but usually listed with them in catalogues, this is 40–45 cm (16–18 in) tall with sizeable cream-coloured flowers, flushed purple outside and with pinkish margins to the petals. Southern France.

T. neustreuvae

Relatively new to our gardens, this is only 10–15 cm (4–6 in) in height with short glossy green leaves and bright yellow flowers 3–5 cm (1¼–2 in) across, shaded with green on the outside. It is one of the easiest of the dwarf species. Central Asia.

T. praestans

This distinctive, stocky, 25–35 cm (10–14 in) tall tulip has broad grey upright leaves and up to five medium-sized flowers in uniform bright orange-red. 'Fusilier' is a good vigorous selection. Central Asia.

T. saxatilis

This lovely, unusual species is ideal for a hot sunny position with space enough to form patches, for it is stoloniferous. The broad, glossy, bright green leaves are

overtopped by 20–35 cm (8–14 in) stems carrying two to four bright pink, yellow-centred flowers 6–8 cm (2½–3⅛ in) across. *T. bakeri* is similar but slightly smaller in flower and habit; a fine selection of this with bright purplish-pink flowers is called 'Lilac Wonder'. Both Crete.

T. sprengeri

The season ends with *T. sprengeri*, a superb tulip 30–45 cm (12–18 in) in height with narrow glossy green leaves and slender brilliant red, gold-backed flowers, which do not open until very late spring or early summer. Although this does not form clumps, it has fat seed pods and is one tulip that will naturalize if left alone. I have seen it thriving in conditions as diverse as hot sunny borders, a shaded woodland with hellebores and erythroniums, and in rough grass. Turkey.

T. sylvestris

Although this is very easy to cultivate, spreading to form patches in sun or dryish semi-shade, it is not very free-flowering. The narrow leaves and 25–40 cm (10–16 in) stems

give it a slender appearance, and the fragrant yellow flowers open to only 6–8 cm (2½–3⅛ in), so it is quite graceful and well worth trying. Western Asia, Europe and a rare British native.

T. tarda

Perhaps the best of all the small species, producing a rosette of leaves on the ground and flattish flowers 5–6 cm (2–2½ in) across, which could be described either as white with a large yellow centre or as yellow with white tips to the petals. It is only 8–10 cm (3⅛–4 in) high when in flower. Central Asia.

T. urumiensis

Another of the excellent dwarf species tulips, with a bunch of narrow dark green leaves at ground level and 10 cm (4 in) stems, each carrying one or two starry bright yellow flowers 5–7 cm (2–2¾ in) across. Iran.

Tulipa hybrids

In this grouping of the hybrids I have not referred to the flowering season in months, since this has little meaning when one considers the enormous range or conditions under which people garden around the world! Instead, I have referred to them as early, mid and late season, bearing in mind that the tulip season as a whole covers the mid to late spring period. There are a great many cultivars and I have picked just a few of each, as a personal selection. The current bulb catalogues list an ever-changing range in all their colourful glory but some stay with us as firm favourites from year to year, and I have tended to recommend these.

Opposite: Grey grasses make an excellent neutral foil for the gaudier dwarf tulips. The dwarf *T. greigii* is a good container plant for mid-spring, here seen next to *Festuca glauca*.
Left: *Tulipa urumiensis* growing through prostrate *Euphorbia myrsinites*.

1. Single early

Early- to mid-season tulips, stocky plants under 40 cm (16 in) tall, which stand up to the weather well and have tubby, rounded flowers.

'Apricot Beauty' – soft apricot-pink, darker inside

'Bellona' – bright golden yellow

'Couleur Cardinal' – bright crimson, shaded purple outside

'Prinses Irene' – pale orange with flame-shaped violet markings

2. Double early

Double equivalents of the above, early to mid-season, mostly under 30 cm (12 in) tall with tightly double flowers.

'Orange Nassau' – deep red graduating to a paler red at the edges

'Peach Blossom' – deep rosy pink

'Schoonoord' – pure white

3. Triumph

Single tulips flowering slighty later than the single early types, mostly taller, at 40–50 cm (16–20 in), but still stout and weather-resistant. They are now often grouped together with the mainly superseded Mendel tulips under the name 'mid-season' tulips.

'African Queen' – deep reddish-purple outlined in white

'Athleet' – pure snowy white

'Attila' – mid violet with paler centre

'Cassini' – deep red throughout

Right: The tulip cultivars are often used for spectacular formal bedding displays but are delightful when used informally in sunny spots between perennials and shrubs. 'Athleet' (white) and 'Prinses Irene' are seen here with *Cytisus praecox* and *Elaeagnus*.

Opposite: The lily-flowered tulips are very graceful and come in a wide range of colours. 'Maytime' harmonizes well with *Erysimum* 'Bowles' Mauve'.

4. Darwin hybrids

A splendid group of mid-season tulips, which I find tend to be more permanent in the garden than most. They have stems 55–65 cm (22–26 in) tall with large oval flowers and bold, grey-green leaves. They are hybrids between the now seldom-cultivated Darwins and *T. fosteriana*.

'Apeldoorn's Elite' – scarlet-red with broad yellow margins
'Beauty of Apeldoorn' – bright yellow, speckled with orange-red
'Elizabeth Arden' – salmon-pink, flushed deeper violet outside

5. Single late

Late-spring tulips with tall stems (60–85 cm/2–2¾ ft) and large rounded flowers, very popular for bedding schemes. They include those that were known as Darwin and Cottage tulips.

'Clara Butt' – salmon-pink, an old favourite
'Georgette' – three to five flowers per stem, with yellow petals edged with red
'Queen of the Night' – deep maroon with a silk-like sheen
'Shirley' – creamy-white edged with purple

6. Lily-flowered

Currently very popular for their elegant flowers, with long-pointed petals tending to turn outwards at the tips. They are medium-tall (45–60 cm/18 in–2 ft) and late-flowering.

'Aladdin' – scarlet-red, edged with yellow
'China Pink' – rich rose-pink
'Maytime' – reddish-purple with narrow white margins
'West Point' – yellow throughout, with very long outcurved tips
'White Triumphator' – pure white

7. Fringed

A late-flowering group, 45–60 cm/
18 in–2 ft) tall with the flowers fringed
with crystal-like outgrowths.
'Blue Heron' – violet-blue with a paler
fringe
'Fancy Frills' – deep pink, paler outside
with a whitish fringe
'Swan Wings' – pure white

8. Viridiflora

Late-flowering, stiff-stemmed, stocky tulips
30–40 cm (12–16 in) tall with curiously
coloured flowers having green shading in
the centre of each of the petals.
'Artist' – salmon-pink with green and
purple shading
'Greenland' – rich pink with green
triangular markings
'Humming Bird' – yellow with a broad,
bright green band
'Spring Green' – pale creamy-yellow with
green markings

9. Rembrandt

Few varieties are now offered, and those that
are available are sometimes grouped with the
single late group. They are about 60–70 cm
(2–2⅓ ft) tall, late-flowering with large flowers
having bright splashes and streaks on a paler
ground colour.
'Sorbet' – opening white, developing
feathery rosy-red markings

10. Parrot

Huge bowl-like flowers with wavy petals,
jagged at the edges and in rich colours,
often with fantastic splashes and streaks of
contrasting colours. They are late-flowering
and 50–60 cm (20 in–2 ft) tall.

'Black Parrot' – deep velvety purple-black
'Fantasy' – bright pink with green splashes
'Flaming Parrot' – creamy-yellow, striped
and feathered crimson

11. Double late

Mid- to late-season double tulips with large
flowers on 45–55 cm (18–22 in) stems,
often known as the 'Peony-flowered' group.
'Allegretto' – bright red, all the petals edged
with yellow
'Angélique' – rose with paler margins,
yellow inside at the base
'Mount Tacoma' – pure white with green
splashes outside

12. *Kaufmanniana* hybrids

These are derived from *T. kaufmanniana*
and are very early-flowering with the same
dwarf habit (12–20 cm/4¾–8 in), short,
broad, grey upright leaves and goblet- to
funnel-shaped flowers in an array of bright
colours, often with a contrasting darker red
band on the outside. Some are hybrids with
T. greigii and have purple-streaked leaves
from that species.
'Johann Strauss' – white inside with yellow
centre, red outside
'Shakespeare' – rich carmine-red, paler
salmon at the edges
'Stresa' – bright yellow with a broad
triangular red mark outside

13. *Fosteriana* hybrids

Mid-season tulips, fairly stocky at
25–40 cm (10–16 in) in height with broad
grey-green leaves and large, rather angular-
oblong flowers; they are selections and
hybrids of *T. fosteriana*.
'Candela' – clear yellow with black stamens
'Orange Emperor' – clear orange, close to a
carrot colour
'Purissima' – opening creamy, changing to
pure white

14. *Greigii* hybrids

Derived from *T. greigii*, these are 15–35 cm
(6–14 in) tall, and most have the broad,
purple-mottled leaves of the species.
'Plaisir' – carmine with creamy edges,
strongly marked leaves
'Red Riding Hood' – bright scarlet with
gorgeous foliage
'Toronto' – unusual in having two to three
red flowers on each stem

Bulbs can play a great role in enhancing the summer border with their contrasting shapes. Here *Allium christophii*, nodding purple *Allium cernuum* and more formal Asiatic lilies are associated with poppies and hardy perennials.

HIGH SUMMER:
CONSIDER THE LILIES, AND OTHER SUMMER BULBS

LILIUM – THE TRUE LILIES

The lilies are among the largest and most graceful of all bulbs and are highly rewarding, since they flower over a fairly long period compared with most bulbous plants. By choosing a range of different types, you can have them in flower from early summer until the autumn, and they are available in a remarkable range of sizes, colours and flower shapes – from the small turk's caps to the large trumpet lilies and the late-summer Oriental types. On the whole, they are not difficult to cultivate and the majority will grow in a well-drained soil that has a good humus content, with plenty of moisture available through the summer growing period. Top dressing the plants with a layer of well-rotted organic matter helps to retain moisture and is very beneficial, since many lilies have feeding roots on the stem just above the bulb. Liquid feeds also help to maintain vigour.

The old saying that lilies need their feet in the shade and their heads in the sun is very true, and often in the wild they can be seen growing up through other plants into the light; so, in the

The Madonna lily, *L. candidum*, is one of the earliest of the lilies, seen here in a traditional cottage garden with lavender.

garden, a site among dwarf shrubs is a natural choice. Most lilies will grow on alkaline soils, provided that there is a good humus content, but some are more lime-tolerant than others, including *L. amabile, L. candidum, L. cernum, L. chalcedonicum, L. henryi, L. pardalinum* and *L. pomponium.*

In gardens where the lily species do not thrive naturally it is well worth trying the Asiatic hybrids, which are on the whole much easier to please than the species. If they just refuse to grow well in the open garden, then try them in large pots or containers, (see page 24) since they will often grow beautifully in these, with very little trouble.

Lily bulbs can be purchased in late autumn or early spring; the former is probably the best season to plant, since it gives time for the roots to become established before the winter, but, provided that good-quality bulbs are obtained, quite

good results. can be achieved by planting in early spring The Madonna lily, L. *candidum*, is an exception, since it starts to grow leaves in the autumn, so it is essential to plant this early, at the end of summer. Because of their size, lilies should be planted with the bulbs 20–25 cm (8–10 in) apart, in the case of the very large ones, and 10–15 cm (4–6 in) apart for the smaller species.

Associations: With the vast range of lily species and hybrids now available, varying widely in colour as well as in form, one is spoilt for choice when it comes to selecting which to grow in a particular position, so I will mention just a few combinations that have 'worked' in my garden. Orange or red lilies and purple foliage plants produce a very striking effect; I achieved this both with the Asiatic hybrid 'Fireking' and *Rosa glauca* (*R. rubrifolia*), and with the very vigorous orange *L. henryi* and the dark

purple-leaved version of *Cotinus coggygria.* Yellow and white lilies – the vigorous Asiatic hybrids are excellent – can be combined in a light, cool display with Bowles' golden grass (*Milium effusum* 'Aureum') and spiky yellow *Sisyrinchium striatum.* Another favourite combination is the white regal lily with the hardy blue *Agapanthus.* If lilies are grown in containers, these experimental associations need not be permanent; one great benefit of growing them in pots is that they can be moved around the garden while in flower to positions where they look good, then stored away in a less conspicuous place.

In the descriptions below, the flower shapes are referred to as trumpet-shaped (these are held nearly horizontally), turk's cap shaped (petals reflexed or rolled backwards, held in a pendent position), or cup-shaped to flattish (facing upwards or outwards).

L. auratum

This magnificent species, the golden-rayed lily of Japan, has wiry stems 1–2 m (3¼–6½ ft) in height carrying five to ten fragrant saucer-shaped flowers 20–30 cm (8–12 in) across, normally white with a yellow band along the centre of each segment and spotted crimson. It really needs a lime-free soil. Japan.

L. bulbiferum

The orange lily grows 1–1.5 m (3¼–5 ft) in height with leafy stems bearing several cup-shaped, upright reddish-orange flowers, spotted darker inside. Its variety *croceum* has small bulbils in the leaf axils and orange flowers without a reddish tint. Europe.

L. canadense

A very graceful lily 90–120 cm (3–4 ft) high with its leaves in whorls and a few elegant pendent bell-shaped yellow, orange or red flowers, which have outward-curving petals, often spotted inside with dark purple. It has curious rhizome-like bulbs. Eastern North America.

L. candidum

The Madonna lily is unusual in that it produces a bunch of leaves at ground level in the autumn and makes most of its growth in winter and spring, flowering sooner than most lilies, in early summer. It has up to fifteen white fragrant, widely funnel-shaped flowers on stiff 1–1.2 m (3¼–4 ft) stems, which carry rather short erect leaves. The best plantings seem to be associated with well-drained rich, neutral or alkaline soils in sheltered sunny situations. Eastern Mediterranean.

L. chalcedonicum

The 'red martagon of Constantinople' is a dramatic turkscap lily with brilliant glossy red flowers on 1–1.2 m (3¼–4 ft) stems, which have many short, upright, silver-margined leaves. It prefers sunny positions and alkaline soils. *L.* × *testaceum*, the Nankeen lily, is an ancient hybrid between this and *L. candidum*, with widely funnel-shaped apricot-coloured flowers; it needs similar conditions to its parents. *L. chalcedonicum* is a native of Greece.

L. duchartrei

A curious species in that its bulbs produce stolons, so that it may appear in a different place each year. The wiry stems are 90–100 cm (3–3¼ ft) in height with narrow leaves and up to twelve small white turk's cap flowers, which have purple spots and streaks. It requires dappled shade in a humus-rich soil. *L. wardii* is very similar to this but the flowers are pinkish-purple with dark spots. Both China.

L. formosanum

A tall, graceful plant up to 1.5 m (5 ft) in height, bearing between one and ten slender 12–18 cm (4¾–7 in) long funnel-shaped fragrant flowers, which are white-stained with wine purple outside. It is somewhat frost-tender but is excellent as a pot plant in a slightly heated glasshouse or conservatory. There is a hardier dwarf form, var. *pricei*, which has solitary flowers on 10–20 cm (4–8 in) stems, and this will tolerate light frosts. Taiwan.

L. hansonii

A martagon lily relative, similar in appearance, with whorls of leaves on the 1–1.5 m (3¼–5 ft) stem, and a raceme of small turk's cap-shaped flowers, which are thick and waxy in texture and orange-yellow, spotted with brown. Take-shima Island, between Japan and Korea.

L. henryi

This is a very robust, easily pleased and long-lived species with tough stems up to 2.5 m (8¼ ft) tall carrying broad, shiny green leaves and ten to twenty large, pendent orange turk's cap flowers on long horizontal stalks; the petals have many prominent hair-like papillae in their lower parts. China.

L. lancifolium (L. tigrinum)

The tiger lily is an old favourite, with up to twenty pendent, orange, dark-spotted turk's cap-shaped flowers. Its 1–1.7 m (3¼–5½ ft) stems have many narrow leaves, which bear small dark bulbils in their axils. Some variations have been named, including var. *flaviflorum*, with yellow flowers; var. *fortunei*, orange-red; *splendens*, a vigorous large-flowered orange one; and a double-flowered monstrous form known as 'Flore Pleno'. China.

L. longiflorum

This is the common white trumpet lily seen in florists' shops, also known as the Easter lily and Bermuda lily. It grows up to 1 m (3¼ ft) in height, with shiny deep-green leaves and one to five pure-white, funnel-shaped, deliciously fragrant flowers 15–20 cm (6–8 in) long. It is very tender, so in cold-winter countries it needs to be grown in the protection of a heated glasshouse. Ryukyu islands.

Right: The beautiful *Lilium mackliniae* was discovered by Frank Kingdon Ward whilst searching for crashed American warplanes in Burma. It needs a cool growing position.

Opposite top: *Lilium pumilum*, a small-flowered but brilliant and easily cultivated turk's cap lily.
Bottom: Perhaps the best of all lily species, the heavily scented *Lilium regale*. It grows well in the garden and is a superb container plant.

L. mackliniae

An unusual and beautiful species with pendent 5 cm (2 in) long bell-like flowers quite unlike those of any other lily, up to five of them being produced on a 20–80 cm (8 in–2⅗ ft) stem. Although basically white, they are flushed pinkish-purple outside. Burma.

L. martagon

The turk's cap lily is a modest species of quiet charm, which prefers the dappled shade under deciduous trees or shrubs. It is 1.5–2 m (5–6½ ft) in height, with whorls of leaves and up to thirty or more small pinkish flowers with darker spots. There is an attractive white form, var. *album*, and a very dark purple, var. *cattaniae* (var. *dalmaticum*). Europe.

L. nepalense

A wonderful lily up to 1.2 m (4 ft) tall, requiring a sheltered but moist situation in summer, when it will produce one to three large pendent bells with recurved tips, greenish-yellow and stained deep maroon on the inside. Nepal.

L. pardalinum

An unusual lily in requiring moist humus-rich growing conditions. The leopard lily grows to about 1.8 m (nearly 6 ft) tall and creeps slowly by means of its rhizome-like bulbs to form patches. It has whorls of leaves and numerous large pendent turk's cap-shaped flowers, which are heavily blotched and speckled purple on a yellow-orange ground colour, shading to red towards the tips of the petals. The similar *L. superbum*, the swamp lily, can reach 3 m (9¾ ft) in height and have as many as forty large flowers with elegantly pointed petals, orange with reddish tips and a central greenish star. *L. pardalinum* is Californian, *L. superbum* is from the eastern United States.

L. pomponium

This very striking scarlet turk's cap lily grows best in a warm position on an alkaline soil. Its slender 30–90 cm (12 in–3 ft) stems carry numerous narrow leaves and small but brilliant, waxy pendent flowers. Maritime Alps.

L. pumilum (L. tenuifolium)

Similar to *L. pomponium*, this is much easier to grow, although not a long-lived plant, and it is necessary to buy or raise new bulbs from time to time. It has very narrow grassy leaves on wiry stems only 40–50 cm (16–20 in) tall and up to twenty fragrant, pendent waxy red turk's cap flowers. 'Golden Gleam' is a yellow-flowered form. China, Tibet.

L. pyrenaicum

A very hardy and easily cultivated lily, 60–100 cm (2–3¼ ft) tall, which is perhaps best used for naturalizing in grass or between shrubs. Normally, the two to ten pendent turk's caps are greenish-yellow streaked with black towards the centre, but there is a sought-after orange-red form, var. *rubrum*. Pyrenees.

L. regale

This is the one lily I would never wish to be without. It is a superb and easily cultivated plant with up to ten large (15 cm/6 in long), deliciously fragrant, funnel-shaped flowers on wiry, weather-resistant stems up to 2 m (6½ ft) in height, which are clothed with many long narrow leaves. Normally the white flowers are suffused purple on the outside, but there is a wholly white form, 'Album'. It will take acid or alkaline conditions and is easily raised from seed. China.

L. speciosum

For the late summer it is worth growing this gorgeous lily, which must rate as one of the most attractive, although in some areas it flowers so late that it can be caught by early frosts. The 1.5–1.7 m (5–5½ ft) stems have scattered, leathery deep-green leaves and five to ten large pendent, fragrant turk's cap flowers, which are white or pale pink, stained and spotted carmine in the centre with conspicuous hair-like papillae. 'Album' is pure white, and 'Rubrum' a stronger carmine with paler edges. *L. speciosum* needs humus-rich conditions. Japan.

Lily hybrids

There are now many superb garden hybrids available to us, thanks to the skill of plant breeders over the last half-century. With so many thousands now listed, it could be chaotic trying to refer to them but, fortunately for gardeners, there is an internationally agreed system of classification for these hybrids, which divides them into eight groups, known as Divisions, largely based on flower shape and parentage. Most of the really excellent garden lilies belong to Divisions I, IV, VI and VII, so I have chosen a selection of cultivars from these groups.

Division I – the Asiatic hybrids

The 'Asiatics' are one of the most popular groups of lilies, both as easy garden plants and as cut flowers. Their flowers vary considerably depending upon the parentage, so three sub-groups are recognized, with the flowers upward-facing, outward-facing or pendent (turk's cap-type).

'Citronella' – pendent turk's caps, yellow, spotted brown
'Connecticut King'– upward-facing, bright yellow, unspotted
'Corsage' – outward-facing, creamy-yellow and pastel-pink mixture
'Enchantment' – upward-facing, bright orange-red with black spots
'Fire King' – outward-facing, deep reddish orange, spotted purple
'Sterling Star' – upward-facing, starry white with dark spots

Division IV – the American hybrids

The North American turk's cap species have

resulted in some striking, tall, very vigorous hybrids that do well in slightly damper situations. They have whorled leaves like the parents and large, pendent, brightly coloured, turk's cap flowers with elegantly recurved petals.

'Bellingham Hybrids' – yellow to orange-red, spotted darker red

Division VI – the trumpet hybrids

The lovely large fragrant trumpet lilies are excellent for containers or the open garden, very vigorous with stout stems 1.5–2 m (5–6½ ft) tall and flowers as much as

15 cm (6 in) long, sometimes twenty to thirty per stem.

'African Queen' – variable apricot-orange, stained bronze outside
'Bright Star' – wide open, creamy with a central orange star
'Golden Splendor' – golden yellow, suffused with purple outside
'Green Dragon' – white, suffused lime-green outside
'Pink Perfection' – varying shades of deep purplish-pink

Division VII – the Oriental hybrids

These are derived from *L. auratum* and *L. speciosum*, with the vigorous *L. henryi* also involved in some. Their very fragrant flowers are usually flattish with the petals recurved, mostly with hair-like projections on the inside.

'Black Beauty' – dark maroon pendent turk's caps, very vigorous
'Casa Blanca' – huge white flattish flowers with brown stamens
'Imperial Gold' – white with a yellow stripe on each petal
'Journey's End' – rich crimson, edged white and spotted crimson
'Stargazer' – upright crimson flowers, paler margins and crimson spots

Top: There are hundreds of Asiatic lily hybrids, many of them derived from the Mid-Century hybrids raised in the Oregon Bulb Farms of Jan de Graaff. There is a wide range of colours and flower shapes to suit any purpose.
Bottom: The pendent Asiatic hybrid lilies are particularly graceful.

OTHER SUMMER BULBS

The lilies may be some of the most spectacular of all summer bulbs, but it should not be forgotten that there are many others which flower at this time that are well worth planting. So we shall now look at some of the best bulbs for bringing colour and interest to the summer garden.

Acidanthera

This deliciously fragrant *Gladiolus* may still be found under its old name. It is frost-tender, but it is really little trouble to lift the corms and store them dry for the winter. I prefer to plant the corms in late spring in pots under glass as a temporary measure, just to get them off to a quick start, otherwise they take a long time to reach the flowering stage and may not do so before the first frosts of autumn. Choose a warm sunny site with plenty of humus to retain the moisture, since this is a plant that requires plenty of water while in growth.

Associations: The best effect I have achieved with *Acidanthera* was a clump of closely planted – almost touching – corms on the sunny side of a silvery conifer, which protected it from the wind and acted as an excellent background to the elegant white flowers.

A. bicolor (Gladiolus callianthus)
This grows to about 1 m (3¼ ft) with bold sword-shaped leaves and a spike of pure white fragrant flowers, which are almost regular in shape, six-petalled with a long arching tube, and with a purple patch in

the cente. The cultivar 'Murielae' may be slightly more robust but is very similar. Tropical African mountains.

Allium

The alliums, which include such culinary delights as garlic, onion, leek, chives and shallots, are a fascinating large group of plants with many attractive species, although there are also a great number of weedy ones that should be avoided. They are characterized by having smallish starry to bell-shaped flowers in umbels at the top of wiry stems, and their leaves and bulbs all have a distinctive onion smell. There are alliums to suit almost any purpose, from small rock-garden species to large border plants. The following selection gives an idea of the range but, if the 'onion bug' strikes, there are many more to experiment with.

They are best obtained and planted in autumn, although some of the small alpine species can be bought in pots for planting at any time. A well-drained sunny situation suits most of them and they are hardy enough to be left undisturbed for as long as they are thriving.

Associations: With such a wide range of types there are many possibilities for experimentation. The tall purple 'drumstick' alliums look excellent growing amid greyish and other ornamental grasses such as *Stipa gigantea*, and I have grown, to great effect, the white form of *A. carinatum* subsp. *pulchellum* with small hardy blue *Agapanthus*, flowering together in late summer.

A. aflatunense
This is one of the best and easiest of the 'drumstick' types, with masses of starry purple flowers in large spherical umbels 10–12 cm (4–4¾ in) in diameter on stout stems up to 1 m (3¼ ft). The true wild species is rare, but the plant distributed under this name, now known as *A. hollandicum*, is similar and a good garden plant. *A. stipitatum* has the same overall appearance, and there is a white form that stands out well against dark backgrounds. All central Asia.

The spherical heads of the 'drumstick' alliums from central Asia provide another dimension in the early summer border. Here, they are combined with a *Ceanothus* and *Stipa gigantea*.

Right: The graceful *Allium carinatum pulchellum* seeds itself freely; here, the white form is spreading beneath a purple-leaved *Rosa glauca*.

Opposite: The attractive leaves of the dwarf *Allium karataviense* show up well when it is grown without too much competition.

A. amabile

A small clump-forming species 10–15 cm (4–6 in) tall with tufts of narrow grassy leaves and small umbels of funnel-shaped reddish-pink flowers. *A. mairei* is very similar. China.

A. atropurpureum

A very dark-flowered species, growing up to 1 m (3¼ ft) in height, with flat-topped hemispherical umbels 4–7 cm (1½–2¾ in) across of many deep-purple starry flowers. Europe.

A. beesianum

Of the smaller species, this is one of the most attractive, only 11–20 cm (4⅓–8 in) in height, forming clumps of narrow leaves and few-flowered umbels of pendent blue bells. It needs a cool position with plenty of humus and will not thrive in warm dryish soils. *A. sikkimense* is very similar but with smaller flowers. Both China.

A. caesium

There are not a great many blue-flowered species of allium, especially of the

'drumstick' type, so this one is of particular interest. It is about 50–60 cm (20 in–2 ft) tall with many powdery blue to violet-blue cup-shaped flowers in umbels 3–5 cm (1¼–2 in) in diameter. *A. caeruleum* (*A. azureum*) is very similar for garden purposes. North and central Asia.

A. carinatum subsp. pulchellum (A. pulchellum)

This late-summer species is most useful in the more natural areas of the garden (a euphemism for the weedier parts!), since it will seed itself around quite freely, but is most attractive, and unwanted clumps are easily pulled out. The wiry 30–40 cm (12–16 in) stems bear medium-sized umbels of bell-shaped purple, pendent flowers on slender stalks, which turn upwards in seed. The white form, 'Album', stands out even better and is a particular favourite of mine. Europe.

A. cernuum

A clump-forming plant producing tufts of narrow leaves and 15–30 cm (6–12 in) stems bearing loose, 3–5 cm (1¼–2 in) diameter pendent umbels of pale pink to deep-purple bell-shaped flowers with protruding stamens. White forms also occur. It is very easily cultivated and will seed itself around. North America.

A. christophii (A. albopilosum)

One of the 'drumstick' types, although it has much larger, looser umbels than most. It is 20–45 cm (8–18 in) in height with impressive, perfectly spherical umbels 15–25 cm (6–10 in) in diameter of starry shiny purple flowers, which become dry and spiny and are valuable for dried winter decorations. Central Asia.

A. cyaneum

A small species suitable for a cool position in humus-rich soil, where it will not dry out too much in summer. The 10–15 cm (4–6 in) stems carry few-flowered umbels of pendent blue bells in late summer. China.

A. cyathophorum var. farreri

This is so easy to grow and seeds so freely that it may be regarded by some as a pest, but it is useful for late summer at the front of perennial borders, being only 15–25 cm (6–10 in) in height. The bell-shaped flowers are reddish-purple, carried in small umbels. China.

A. flavum

An elegant easily cultivated species, variable in size from 5 to 30 cm (2–12 in) in height and unusual in being one of the few yellow-flowered alliums. It has narrow grey leaves and wiry stems bearing loose umbels of small pale- to deep-yellow bell-shaped flowers on long stalks, which are pendent, then turning upwards when in seed. Some forms are pleasantly fragrant. Europe, western Asia.

A. giganteum

One of the largest species, 1–2 m (3¼–6½ ft) tall with broad basal leaves and stout stems carrying large spherical umbels 10–15 cm (4–6 in) across, containing hundreds of individually small starry lilac-purple flowers. It requires a hot sunny position, protected from late frosts, which can damage the leaves. *A. macleanii* (*A. elatum*) is rather similar. Both central Asia. Hybrid alliums with the same general appearance, but even more vigorous and dramatic with large umbels, include 'Beau Regard' and 'Lucy Ball'.

A. karataviense

This is among my favourite alliums. Very striking although only 15–20 cm (6–8 in) in height, it has 15–20 cm (6–8 in) wide umbels of pale pink starry flowers, set between two or three beautiful broad, grey-purple leaves. I have it in the gravel of our driveway, where it appears to thrive on the sharp drainage and is effective away from the competition of other plants. Central Asia.

A. moly

Although commonly cultivated and cheap to buy, this is quite unusual among the alliums in being yellow-flowered. It is 15–25 cm (6–10 in) in height with broad grey leaves and hemispherical umbels 5–7 cm (2–2¾ in) across of starry golden-yellow flowers, each about 1–1.5 cm (½–⅝ in) in diameter. It is very easy to please in semi-shade or sun and is useful for naturalizing beneath deciduous shrubs. France, Spain.

A. narcissiflorum

A beautiful alpine clump-forming species 15–25 cm (6–10 in) in height with a few narrow leaves and small umbels of pendent pinkish-purple bells, large for an allium at 1–1.5 cm (½–⅝ in) long. It requires a sunny position, but one that is well supplied with moisture throughout its summer growing season. *A. insubricum* is very similar, but with fewer, larger flowers in the umbel. Northern Italy, southern France.

A. neapolitanum

In cold areas this needs a sheltered sunny position if it is to thrive. It is slender, 20–30 cm (8–12 in) tall with narrow leaves and wiry stems bearing loose umbels 5–7 cm (2–2¾ in) across of large, glistening white saucer-shaped flowers that last well in water. A good form of this is sold as *A. cowanii.* Mediterranean region.

A. nigrum

An easily cultivated species, suitable for growing amid perennials in the open border. It is 80–90 cm (2⅔–3 ft) tall with strap-like leaves and a thick stem carrying a flat-topped umbel 8–10 cm (3⅛–4 in) wide, with many large saucer-shaped white flowers, which have a blackish ovary in the centre. It is seldom offered, but *A. multibulbosum* is available more often and is like a vigorous variant of it. Mediterranean region.

A. oreophilum (A. ostrowskianum)

This dwarf species is suitable for a rock garden or raised sunny bed. It is only 5–10 cm (2–4 in) in height with 4–6 cm (1½–2½ in) diameter umbels of deep rose-red flowers. 'Zwanenburg' is a selection with richly coloured flowers. Western and central Asia.

A. paradoxum

In a good form this can be a most attractive plant, but there are variants with mostly bulbils in the umbel rather than flowers. It is 10–25 cm (4–10 in) in height with a small umbel of attractive pendent white bells, each about 1 cm (½ in) long. It is a very easily cultivated species and can be used for naturalizing in semi-shade. Western Asia.

A. roseum

It is best to choose forms of this that have only flowers in the umbel, since some have bulbils as well and are less attractive. It has wiry stems 15–45 cm (6–18 in) tall with loose umbels of clear pink or white cup-shaped flowers, each 1–2 cm (½–¾ in) in diameter. Mediterranean region.

A. rosenbachianum

Like *A. aflatunense* and *A. hollandicum*, this is another 'drumstick' type with strap-like basal leaves and stems up to 80–90 cm (2⅔–3 ft) tall bearing dense spherical umbels 8–10 cm (3⅛–4 in) across. Although small and starry, the many dark purple flowers collectively make a striking show. Central Asia.

A. schoenoprasum (Chives)

A well-known culinary plant, this should not be overlooked as an ornamental. The 10–25 cm (4–10 in) tufts of cylindrical leaves are accompanied by tight shuttlecock-like umbels of pale purple, pink or more rarely white bell-shaped flowers. There are several named selections, but 'Forescate' is particularly good, robust with rich rosy-pink flowers. Europe, Asia.

A. schubertii

To me, this is one of the most entertaining of all the alliums, although it does take up rather a lot of room. Its stem is only about 30–45 cm (12–18 in) tall but the umbel is huge, sometimes 45 cm (18 in) across, with many starry pale purple flowers, although these are widely spaced on stalks of differing lengths and the whole appearance is therefore of a very loose umbel. Middle East.

A. senescens

An attractive patch-forming species with a rhizomatous rootstock and a leafy appearance, since the foliage stays in good condition until flowering time. It is very variable and it is worth seeking the compact forms with grey-green, twisted leaves, since they are quite ornamental. The stems may be anything from 5 to 30 cm (2–12 in) in height, each carrying a dense umbel 2–5 cm (¾–2 in) across of small pale- to deep-pink flowers. It is a very good, easily cultivated plant for the front of borders and the rock garden, attracting many butterflies and bees. Plants sold as *A. montanum* are often dwarf with good foliage. Europe, Asia.

A. sphaerocephalon

A 'drumstick' allium, although this one has much smaller umbels than the large ones such as *A. aflatunense*, only 3–6 cm (1¼–2½ in) in diameter. These are carried on long wiry stems 50–90 cm (20 in–3 ft) tall and have numerous deep-purple bell-shaped flowers. It is very easily cultivated in a sunny spot. Europe, western Asia.

A. unifolium

An attractive species with one curved greyish-green basal leaf and a 15–25 cm (6–10 in) stem carrying a hemispherical umbel 5–6 cm (2–2½ in) in diameter. The flowers are fairly large, each up to 2 cm (¾ in) across, pink and saucer-shaped. A very good form of this is around in cultivation as 'A. murrayanum'. California, Oregon.

Anomatheca

I have retained this name since gardeners will not yet have become used to the idea that it is now regarded as a freesia! The only species widely cultivated is A. laxa, which is almost hardy but occasionally succumbs when the ground is frozen for lengthy periods. A sheltered sunny position suits it best and, when happy, it will seed itself around. The freesia-like corms are obtained and planted in spring.

Associations: Although not showy, this bulb can be useful for providing summer interest in a sunny bed where there are dormant autumn-flowering bulbs, such as nerines and *Amaryllis*.

A. laxa (Freesia laxa, Lapeirousia cruenta)

This produces fans of narrow sword-shaped leaves and 10–30 cm (4–12 in) stems bearing short spikes of 2–3 cm (¾–1¼ in) diameter red flowers, which have a darker blotch in the centre. The white form, 'Alba', and the blue-flowered subsp. *azurea* are worthwhile variants. South Africa.

Arisaema

This large and increasingly popular group of hardy aroids – members of the *Arum*, or cuckoo pint, family – has large, elegantly divided leaves and cowl-like hooded spathes, mostly chocolate-coloured, green or occasionally white, from which protrudes a pencil-, club- or whip-like 'spadix'. The tubers are best planted in spring and, in the case of those described below, may be left in the ground throughout the winter months while they are dormant. A soil well supplied with organic matter is best, since this will have the moisture-retaining properties essential for these summer growers. Many produce heads of bright red berries in late summer to early autumn. Unlike many of the hardy aroids, the spathes of arisaemas are not smelly!

Associations: Arisaemas, at least the Asiatic ones, are often found growing with rhododendrons in the wild and these also make excellent garden companions, the arisaemas providing summer interest when most of the rhododendrons are finished.

A. candidissimum

Arguably the best of them all, this has beautiful white or pink-and-green striped 15 cm (6 in) long spathes, which overtop the developing foliage, but then the large three-lobed leaves expand to 30 cm (12 in) or more across. It will grow in sun or dappled shade and is very hardy. China.

A. consanguineum

A very vigorous species 1 m (3¼ ft) or more tall, with an ornamental blotched stem bearing a large leaf that is divided into many slender leaflets radiating out like the spokes of an umbrella. The purple or green, often striped, spathe is held below the leaf and is about 15–20 cm (6–8 in) long with a whip-like appendage at its tip. Himalayas, China.

A. flavum

Perhaps this is more of a curiosity, since its spathes are small and yellow, which is a very unusual colour in the genus. It is 15–30 cm (6–12 in) tall with leaves made up of five to ten leaflets. The spathe is 3–4 cm (1¼–1½ in) long with the hood sharply folded over so that it almost closes the mouth. Asia, from Arabia to China.

The Chinese *Arisaema candidissimum*, one of the hardiest and most attractive of a fascinating group of aroids.

A. ringens

This has large leaves with three broad leaflets, which taper at the apex to long points. The spathes, which are overtopped by the leaves, are green or purplish with paler stripes and have a curious domed hood at the apex. Eastern Asia.

A. sikokianum

Perhaps one of the most exciting species, this is 30–45 cm (12–18 in) tall with a tubular blackish-purple spathe, which is wide open at the mouth revealing a white, thick, club-like spadix. The leaves follow slightly afterwards and consist of three to five leaflets. It seems to be very hardy, but can be caught by late frosts if it emerges early after a mild spell. Japan.

A. tortuosum

A robust species 60–120 cm (2–4 ft) in height with a stout stem bearing leaves that are attractively divided into up to seventeen finger-like leaflets. The green spathe is somewhat hidden below the leaves and is interesting in that the spadix makes an S-shape as it emerges from the mouth of the spathe. Himalayan region.

A. triphyllum (Jack in the Pulpit)

This is 30–60 cm (1–2 ft) in height with spotted stems carrying leaves with three leaflets and a hooded green spathe, which may be purple-flushed and striped with green or white. It is a very hardy species. North America.

Calochortus

Most of the lovely Calochortus that are cultivated flower in spring and are summer-dormant, so the main description for this genus is found in the chapter on spring bulbs, but there are several Mexican species that behave in reverse, being winter-dormant and flowering in the summer. Only one of these is in general cultivation and this should be planted in spring in a sunny situation, where it will receive plenty of moisture throughout its growing period.

C. barbatus (Cyclobothra lutea)

The slender, loosely branched stems grow 15–30 cm (6–12 in) tall and bear several pendent mustard-yellow bells, which are hairy inside and about 3 cm (1¼ in) across. Mexico.

Cardiocrinum

The giant lily is a close relative of the true lilies and, apart from its colossal size, differs most obviously in having large heart-shaped leaves. Although not difficult to grow when the right conditions are provided, it does require quite a lot of space to grow a group of them, if they are to look 'in place' in the garden. But one might grow a single bulb for fun, just to enjoy the drama. It requires a deep humus-rich soil, which is well supplied with moisture in summer, and it will not thrive in climates with a dry summer atmosphere, so in such areas it may be necessary to apply a fine spray through a sprinkler system during dry periods. The bulbs die after flowering but produce offsets that will eventually also

flower, although it may be three or four years before they do so; seeds take even longer: up to seven years. The bulbs should be planted in autumn or spring with their tips just below the surface of the soil.

Associations: Rhododendrons are often natural associates of the giant lily, and a drift of lilies in the gap between some of these dark-leaved evergreens can be an arresting sight, providing summer interest when the rhododendrons have finished flowering.

C. giganteum

This is the most well-known species and is aptly named, for the overall height of the plant can be as much as 4 m (13 ft), with a basal cluster of huge glossy heart-shaped leaves and a spike of white trumpets up to 15 cm (6 in) long. There are several species, all rather similar and requiring much the same conditions. Himalayas, China.

Crinum

The majority of species in this large, predominantly tropical genus are very tender and require heated glasshouse protection in cool temperate countries, but there are a few that are valuable garden plants in milder areas, since they are large, bold plants suitable for perennial borders. They have large long-necked bulbs producing clusters of broad basal leaves and stout stems in mid to late summer, carrying umbels of large funnel-shaped, fragrant flowers that open in succession. The bulbs

Opposite: The strongly fragrant Crinum moorei from Natal is one of the parents of the widely cultivated C. × powellii.

are planted in spring in an open sunny position in soil that has been worked deeply to accommodate the large bulbs, leaving the tip of the neck just protruding. There should be a good humus content to encourage moisture retention, since they require plenty of water while in growth. In cold areas it is wise to protect the clumps with any loose material, such as bracken, since they can be damaged by prolonged frost.

Associations: With their rather tropical appearance, crinums are quite useful for planting as a perennial feature in borders that are used for exotic summer bedding, particularly if purple-leaved variants of 'foliage' plants such as *Ricinus, Canna* and *Kochia* are used. In cold areas they make impressive container plants, but are best moved under glass for the winter.

C. bulbispermum

A robust winter-deciduous crinum, 60–90 cm (2–3 ft) in height when in flower, having a tuft of grey-green leaves and umbels of between five and fifteen funnel-shaped, sweetly scented white or pinkish flowers 15–20 cm (6–8 in) long; these have a bold reddish 'pyjama' stripe along the centre of each petal. Southern Africa.

C. moorei

A beautiful plant up to 1 m (3¼ ft) in height with a tuft of semi-evergreen broad green leaves and stout purplish flower stems bearing five to ten very widely funnel-shaped flowers with a diameter of 15–20 cm (6–8 in), white or palest shell-pink with a delicate fragrance. Natal, eastern Cape.

C. × powellii

This is an old garden-raised hybrid between the above two species, curiously much tougher, frost-wise, than either of its supposed parents. It is similar to *C. moorei* in growth habit, but the flowers are funnel-shaped and a much stronger shade of pink, with usually five to ten in each umbel on a stout stem 60–100 cm (2–3¼ ft) tall. They are individually about 10 cm (4 in) across at the mouth and are carried on long, gracefully curved tubes. The white version, 'Album', stands out even better, especially if planted against a dark background. Garden origin.

Crocosmia

The old 'Montbretia', *C. × crocosmiiflora*, is often somewhat despised, since it seems to be capable of growing successfully almost anywhere, especially on rubbish dumps, but it does have its uses for this very reason. Some of the modern selections and hybrids are splendid border plants, although in cold areas they are not always very satisfactory. They are best in sunny well-drained positions with plenty of moisture available in summer, so situations that become hot and dry are not suitable. A sandy soil with a good humus content seems to suit them well. Planting can take place in spring as soon as the soil has warmed up; subsequently, in cold winter areas, they are best protected by bracken or something similar, when dormant. They have upright fans of sword-like leaves, overtopped by branching spikes of curved, funnel-shaped flowers that flare out at the mouth.

Associations: With their bright, often fiery, colours and spiky leaves, crocosmias are excellent for providing splashes of colour in mixed borders in mid summer. Try a planting of one of the orange or red cultivars with a drift of the foamy white *Gypsophila paniculata*.

C. x crocosmiiflora

This old hybrid is 40–60 cm (16 in–2 ft) in height with panicles of orange funnel-shaped flowers. It does well in a great range of situations and is particularly useful for dry, even shady, places where many other plants will not thrive. Garden origin.

C. masoniorum

A very robust, elegant species 1–1.5 m (3¼–5 ft) in height with bold pleated leaves and branched stems carrying many reddish-orange, long-tubed flowers 2–3 cm (¾–1¼ in) long, which face upwards from the horizontal branches and have conspicuously protruding stamens. South Africa.

C. paniculata (Curtonus paniculatus)

This is a striking late-summer perennial, up to 1.5 m (5 ft) in height with broad pleated leaves in bold iris-like fans. The tough branched stems bear many long-tubed, orange-red flowers up to 5 cm (2 in) long. South Africa.

Crocosmia cultivars

There are some excellent hybrid cultivars, which combine the hardiness of Montbretia with the vigour and striking colours of the species. A few examples are:

Aptly named *Crocosmia 'Lucifer'* is one of the most brilliant of the summer bulbs, growing here amongst summer perennials.

'Bressingham Blaze' – bright red funnel-shaped flowers, 60–90 cm (2–3 ft)
'Citronella' – a pleasant pale lemon-yellow shade, 40–60 cm (16 in–2 ft)
'Emberglow' – large, glowing orange-red flowers, vigorous, 75 cm (2½ ft)
'Emily McKenzie' – orange with dark brownish-red marks, 50–60 cm (20 in–2 ft)
'Jackanapes' – bicoloured yellow and orange flowers, 50–60 cm (20 in–2 ft)
'Lucifer' – flame-red flowers, about 1 m (3¼ ft)
'Solfatare' – bronzy foliage and yellow flowers, 40–50 cm (16–20 in)

Dierama (Angel's Fishing Rod, Wand Flower)

These are among the most graceful of all 'bulbous' plants, forming clumps of tough, narrow leaves that are almost evergreen. In summer, long, arched wiry stems bear spikes of bell-shaped flowers, which are pendent on thread-like stalks. Although they need warm sunny positions, they also require plenty of moisture in summer. One of the best plantings I have seen was near a garden pool, where they were self-seeding into the cracks between the paving slabs. They can be difficult to get established, and it is best to acquire young plants in pots and to plant them directly into their final positions.

Associations: It is important that surrounding plants are low-growing, or the grace of the dieramas is lost. As mentioned above, they look good in paving but are also highly effective among greyish grasses.

D. dracomontanum (D. pumilum)
One of the smaller species, this may be up to 1 m (3¼ ft) in height but is often much less, making dense 'grassy' clumps overtopped by drooping spikes of pale to deep pink or purple, flared funnel-like flowers 2–2.5 cm (¾–1 in) long. Drakensberg mountains.

D. pendulum
One of the taller species, up to 2 m (6½ ft) in height, with long stems having dangling

Right: *Eucomis comosa*, the pineapple flower, attracts many insects to the late-summer border.

Far right: In frosty areas the elegant galtonias will require lifting for the winter. Shown in front of *Rosa glauca* are the green *G. viridiflora* and white *G. candicans*.

Opposite: There is a gladiolus for every colour scheme. Here, brilliant 'Peter Pears' has been combined with purple foliage.

branches and pendent funnel-shaped purple-pink flowers that flare out widely at the mouth and are 3–5 cm (1¼–2 in) long. South Africa.

D. pulcherrimum

This is the best-known dierama in cultivation and is very similar to *D. pendulum* but has less widely flaring bells, 3.5–5.5 cm (1⅜–2¼ in) long in deep magenta-purple, although the colour varies considerably. It is a wonderfully graceful plant up to 2 m (6½ ft) in height. South Africa.

Eucomis

The pineapple flowers are mostly late-summer-flowering, dying down completely in winter, and are proving to be much hardier than at first suspected, so I am sure we will see more of them in the future. They have rosettes of rather fleshy basal leaves, sometimes wavy at the edges, and dense spikes of starry flowers, crowned at the top by a cluster of small leaf-like bracts. Only a few species are obtainable, but these are probably the best, especially some of the newer selections with more colourful spikes. They can be grown in open sunny positions, as long as they are kept well watered in summer. They also make good container plants for the patio, although the flowers of some of them have a 'cabbage' smell, attracting many insects. The bulbs are best planted in spring.

Associations: These are interesting but not showy, so they stand out best if the associated plants are fairly neutral, for example the blue-grey *Euphorbia wulfenii*, which will have flowered much earlier. A clump of *Eucomis comosa* can also look extremely effective in an area of paving, without the competition of other plants.

E. bicolor

This is one of the most frequently seen, with wavy-margined leaves, purple-blotched stems and stout spikes 30–40 cm (12–16 in) tall of pale green flowers, the petals of which are outlined with purple. Natal.

E. comosa

This, and its selections – perhaps hybrids – is probably the best garden plant of all the species, a robust grower with purple-spotted and -striped flower stems up to 60 cm (2 ft) in height, carrying dense spikes of pale green, pinkish or purplish flowers, which have a deep-purple ovary in the centre forming a dark eye. Some selections have strongly purple-tinted foliage. Eastern Cape, Natal.

E. zambesiaca

The plant that is cultivated under this name is an attractive dwarf one, only 15–25 cm (6–10 in) in height, with wavy leaves and spikes of white flowers. Southern Africa.

Galtonia

Another African genus, with only a few species, but they are valuable garden plants, suitable for growing in a mixed border amid other perennials. They are tall elegant plants with long strap-like leaves and long racemes of pendent green or white bells in mid to late summer. The bulbs should be planted in spring in a sunny position where they will not dry out in summer and, in mild areas, can be left in the ground; however, in cold areas they must be lifted and stored dry for the winter. I prefer to start the bulbs into growth in spring in pots under glass, then plant them out when the soil has warmed up, since this gets them off to a good start.

Associations: An interesting combination arose by chance when my favourite species, the green-flowered *G. viridiflora*, seeded itself in front of the grey-purple foliage of *Rosa glauca*, so you might try this, and the other species, in association with various purple- or grey-leaved plants.

G. candicans
This grows up to 1.5 m (5 ft) or more in height with a loose raceme of twenty to thirty pendent white bells, each about 3 cm (1¼ in) long. It is the most vigorous and is readily available. Eastern Cape, Natal, Lesotho.

G. princeps
A more delicate-looking plant than *G. candicans* with the flowers slightly smaller and tinted with pale green. Natal.

G. viridiflora
I find this most attractive, having soft green flowers, more funnel- than bell-shaped. It is hardier in my garden than either of the others, seeding itself in a sunny, sandy situation. Eastern Cape, Natal, Lesotho.

Gladiolus

A large and much-loved group of summer 'bulbs', of which there are probably as many as 150 wild species, but it is the host of colourful large-flowered hybrids that gives the genus its greatest publicity, both as garden plants for planting out in spring and as cut flowers. The majority have erect, narrow sword-shaped leaves and spikes of funnel-shaped flowers, which curve over to the horizontal and tend to face all in one direction. The upper petal is usually hooded and often there are contrasting marks on the lower petals. The corms of the summer-flowering gladioli are usuallly on sale in spring, but they should not be planted until the soil has begun to warm up, otherwise they may rot before starting into growth. In all but the mildest areas they are then lifted again in the autumn and stored dry and frost-free for the winter. Very few of the wild species of summer-flowering *Gladiolus* are cultivated, but one or two are available. There are, however, a large number of interesting but tender winter- or early spring-flowering ones from South Africa, which make their growth through the winter months and in cold areas require a frost-free greenhouse or conservatory. These are gaining in popularity with enthusiasts, although they are at present difficult to obtain, but some are available and I have mentioned them in the chapter on Cape bulbs.

Associations: The large gladiolus cultivars, with their stiffly erect leaves and flower spikes, have a very rigid appearance and are ideal for formal planting schemes, but they can be quite effective in small groups among herbaceous perennials, especially the smaller-flowered cultivars and the more delicate-looking 'Nanus' varieties. The pink and purplish shades of gladiolus are especially effective with silvery foliage, as are blood-red gladiolus with purple-leaved plants.

Hardier than the large-flowered hybrids, the *nanus* gladiolus are also smaller and more graceful.

G. communis subsp. *byzantinus*

Unlike most of the gladiolus we grow in our gardens, which are derived from South African species, this is a hardy Mediterranean species that can be left in the ground to form clumps. The corms are planted in autumn in a sunny position and will flower in early summer, about 60–90 cm (2–3 ft) in height with spikes of rich reddish-purple flowers. Mediterranean region.

G. italicus (G. segetum)

In its native areas this is often a weed of cornfields, colouring the fields magenta-pink. It can be grown successfully in a warm sunny position and is worth having for its 50–70 cm (20 in–2⅓ ft) spikes of small but richly coloured flowers. The corms are planted in autumn. Mediterranean region.

G. papilio (G. purpureoauratus)

One of the hardiest of all gladiolus and perhaps cultivated more as a curiosity than for show, although some like its muted colours. It is 80–100 cm (2⅗–3¼ ft) in height and has few-flowered spikes of strongly hooded flowers in a strange mixture of green, pale purple and yellow, produced in late summer or early autumn. The corms produce stolons, so it can form large colonies and should be planted where it can be left undisturbed. South Africa.

Gladiolus cultivars

The hybridization of *Gladiolus* species dates back to the early nineteenth century and there are now thousands of varieties, and new ones are appearing all the time. For ease of reference they have been classified by the North American Gladiolus Council into groups according to flower size, and I have chosen just a few from each group as examples.

Giant-flowered group

Flowers over 14 cm (5½ in) in diameter.
'Oscar' – blood-red
'Rose Supreme' – rosy-pink, speckled darker with cream centre
'Traderhorn' – rich deep scarlet-red, white in the throat

Large-flowered group

Flowers under 14 cm (5½ in) in diameter.
'Fidelio' – carmine-purple
'Peter Pears' – apricot-salmon, red-blotched throat
'White Friendship' – pure white

Medium-flowered group

Flowers under 11.5 cm (4½ in) in diameter.
'Green Woodpecker' – greenish-yellow flowers, red in throat
'Violetta' – deep violet

Small-flowered group

Flowers under 9 cm (3½ in) in diameter.
'Bluebird' – medium violet, marked darker violet
'Claret' – medium rosy-red
'Snow Castle' – pure white

Miniature-flowered group

Flowers under 6 cm (2½ in) in diameter.
'Camborne' – lilac, stained darker violet

Butterfly group

These have smallish flowers with striking colours, often with contrasting splashes of colour on the lower petals.
'Avalanche' – pure white
'Chartres' – purple with darker markings
'Dancing Doll' – cream stained pink, red-blotched on lower petals

Primulinus group

These have a flower shape resembling that of the wild species *G. primulinus*, funnel-shaped and strongly hooded, rather few on each spike.
'Columbine' – carmine-pink with a white blotch in the throat
'Lady Godiva' – a good white
'Sabu' – dusky red

Nanus group

These are particular favourites of mine. They are much shorter at about 45–60 cm (18 in–2 ft), with fewer flowers; they flower much earlier; the flowers are smaller; and they are hardier than those of the above groups. The corms are usually available in autumn (sometimes also in spring) and in mild areas are best planted in autumn as soon as purchased. However, in cold areas I think it best to pot them and keep them under cover until spring, then plant them out.
'Amanda Mahy' – salmon with violet spotting
'Nymph' – white with pink markings
'Prins Claus' – white with red blotches
'The Bride' – white with green markings on the lower petals

Habranthus (Rain Lily)

In cool temperate regions these South American bulbs are not hardy, although one or two might be tried in sheltered sunny spots in the milder regions. They have tufts of narrow leaves and, in summer or early autumn, leafless stems with solitary funnel-shaped flowers. In cold areas they are better grown in pots in a frost-free greenhouse or conservatory, keeping them warm and almost completely dry after the leaves have died back. They flower as soon as they are watered after their rest period in spring and early summer.

Associations: It is worth trying a few bulbs in a warm sunny bed amid grey-leaved shrubs such as *Convolvulus cneorum*, which will provide some protection as well as a foil for the flowers.

H. robustus

This is one of the most showy, with large pale-pink funnel-shaped flowers 5–8 cm (2–3⅛ in) long in summer. Brazil, Paraguay.

H. tubispathus (H. andersonii)

It is worth trying this outside in mild gardens since it is probably the hardiest, although not the most spectacular, with rather small funnel-shaped flowers about 3 cm (1¼ in) long. The colour is, however, most attractive, mustard yellow with a coppery or reddish stain on the exterior. The flowers appear sporadically over a long period in late summer. Argentina, Uruguay.

Moraea

Most of the iris-like moraeas are tender winter-growing plants, suitable for a cool conservatory or frost-free greenhouse in cold areas, but there are a few summer-flowering species that do well in an open sunny position. The flowers have three showy outer petals and three smaller inner ones, just like an iris, but they have corms more like a gladiolus. Most of the hardy summer moraeas are clump-forming, with long, narrow, evergreen channelled leaves. They should be planted in spring in a deep rich soil, and given a plentiful supply of moisture throughout their growing and flowering season.

Associations: The summer moraeas are most effective when planted as individuals and left to form dense clumps. Their bright yellow flowers create a splash of colour when placed amid darker-leaved subjects such as rhododendrons, and they seem to enjoy similar conditions, with summer moisture at the roots.

For the autumn months, nothing can surpass a drift of mixed pink and white *Cyclamen hederifolium* in the dappled shade.

A LATE FLUSH OF COLOUR:
BULBS FOR THE AUTUMN

One of the joys of gardening with bulbs is the flush of colour that appears at the end of summer when the rest of the garden is coming to a rusty-brown end and everything is looking a little tired. Some of the best bulbs, and particular favourites of mine, are the autumn crocuses and the similarly shaped but unrelated colchicums, which are often erroneously referred to as autumn crocuses.

It is useful to know the difference, since crocus corms are edible, although not very desirable, while colchicums are highly poisonous! The two can barely be confused, since crocus flowers have only three stamens, whereas colchicums have six and, in leaf, the very narrow crocus leaves have a central pale stripe, quite unlike the broader, stripeless colchicum leaves. One could add that the autumn crocuses are at the bluer end of the spectrum and colchicums at the pinkish end, and so they produce rather different effects. There is therefore a good case for having plenty of both in the garden.

The more robust species and varieties will grow in any reasonable soil – acid or alkaline, and even heavy clay – provided that it does not lie wet and stagnant in summer when they are at rest. Colchicums are also fine in grass, which helps to make up for their bare leafless flowers. The long corms of colchicums need at least 10 cm (4 in) of soil above them.

Associations: Plantings of the more robust colchicums, such as *C. speciosum* and its hybrids, look marvellous when planted in quantity beneath deciduous trees and shrubs (on their sunnier side), such as maples and *Cotinus*, flowering just as the leaves take on their autumn tints; the white form of *C. speciosum* is particularly valuable for this purpose. A favourite combination in my garden is a group of the rosy-coloured *C. cilicicum* beneath the grey-purple *Rosa glauca*, especially when there is a good crop of rosehips as well. In view of their leafless appearance at flowering time, they look best when combined with other plants that have interesting foliage, such as grey artemisias or purple-leaved sage.

C. × agrippinum

A superb early-flowering hybrid with attractive funnel-shaped flowers, strongly chequered dark purple on a rosy-lilac ground colour. It needs a sunny position and will form dense clumps with many flowers when growing well. The narrow, slightly twisted leaves are not as overwhelming as in many of the autumn species and their hybrids. Garden hybrid.

C. autumnale

The meadow saffron has many long-tubed, pinkish-lilac, goblet-shaped flowers in early autumn. Although very floriferous and easily cultivated, its flowers fall over in inclement weather, so it really looks at its best when grown in grass, its natural habitat. Its large, glossy green leaves appear in spring. Various selections have been made, including the white 'Album', the many-petalled white 'Alboplenum' and the double pink 'Pleniflorum'. Europe.

C. bivonae (C. sibthorpii, C. bowlesianum)

A few colchicums have chequered flowers, and this is one of the best, with funnel- to wineglass-shaped flowers in pale pink overlaid with a conspicuous darker purple tessellated pattern. Italy to Turkey.

C. × byzantinum

Like *C. × autumnale*, of which it is probably a hybrid, this has pinkish flowers in early autumn but they are a little larger and it is more floriferous, often several opening all together in a bunch. The leaves come later and are large, but not unattractive, when fully expanded, so it needs plenty of room. Garden hybrid.

C. cilicicum

One of my favourite species, having clusters of warm rosy-coloured large, but short-tubed, flowers that stand up well to wind and rain. The large, striking, glossy leaves appear later on and last until late spring. Turkey.

C. speciosum

Undoubtedly this is the most valuable of the colchicums for garden use, much better than *C. autumnale*, as the flowers are larger and more robustly weather-resistant. They have an elegant goblet shape and are variable in colour, mostly in shades of purple with a conspicuous white zone in the centre. It will grow in sun or dappled shade and is worth planting in quantity, bearing in mind that the bold, shiny green leaves will take up considerable space until summer. The stately pure white form, 'Album', is arguably the finest of all autumn bulbs. Turkey, Caucasus.

C. variegatum

Although rather uncommon in cultivation and not the easiest colchicum to grow well, this is well worth seeking in catalogues since it is strikingly distinct. The flowers, which are conspicuously tessellated purple on a pale-pinkish background, are almost flat when fully open and have short tubes, so that they appear starry and are held only just above the ground. The leaves are small compared with most autumnal colchicums, grey-green and undulate. It needs a warm sunny position. Greek islands, Turkey.

Colchicum hybrids

In addition to the *Colchicum* species described above, many cultivars and hybrids are available, such as: 'Lilac Wonder' (lilac-pink), 'Rosy Dawn' (bright rose, slightly tessellated darker), 'The Giant' (large, mauve with a paler throat), 'Violet Queen' (rich purple without a pale zone in the throat). 'Waterlily'

is a 'double', many-petalled form with several pinkish-lilac flowers produced together in a bunch, very showy, but the flowers are top-heavy and fall over; some people do not object to this, but it is all a matter of taste!

Crocus

The autumn crocuses, although similar in shape to the colchicums, are on the whole smaller and more dainty, growing to only 5–10 cm (2–4 in). Some produce flowers before their leaves and have the same naked appearance, while others, which are perhaps rather more attractive, have the narrow leaves developed to varying degrees. Some of the cheaper, more readily obtainable ones, such as *C. speciosus*, are best planted in quantity in grass or shrub borders for a mass effect. The soil should be reasonably fertile and well drained, but it does not seem to matter whether it is acid or

alkaline. Two species, *C. banaticus* and *C. nudiflorus*, require slightly damper soils, where they will not become too hot and dry in summer while dormant. These autumnal crocuses are planted as soon as they can be obtained in late summer.

Associations: By choosing a range of species it is possible to have a display of autumn crocuses for a few weeks, although individually the flowers are fairly short-lived. Companion plantings must be chosen with care to ensure that the crocuses are not shaded, since their flowers need all the available sun if they are to open properly. Their diminutive size makes them suitable for associating with small perennials and alpines, and the more vigorous species will grow through dwarf plants such as the silvery *Antennaria dioica*, the trailing purple-grey *Sedum cauticolum* and carpeting thymes.

Right: A sunny, well-drained position suits many of the Greek autumn crocuses. Here, *C. goulimyi* 'Mani White', *C. hadriaticus* 'Lilacinus', *C. cancellatus* and *C. tournefortii* grow amid alpines.

Opposite: The true saffron crocus, *C. sativus*, is a gorgeous plant as well as supplying a small quantity of the famous spice from its red stigmas.

C. banaticus

A unique species with lilac-blue flowers, which have three large outer petals and three smaller inner ones, making it rather iris-like. It is also unusual in liking damper positions in partial shade, but with enough sun to encourage the flowers to open. The leaves appear in spring. Romania.

C. cancellatus

This blooms in early autumn before the leaves, with pale blue or white flowers veined darker on the outside and often with attractive orange stigmas. It needs a warm sunny position. Greece, east to Iran.

C. goulimyi

This is a splendid and elegant goblet-shaped crocus, its lilac-blue flowers with a slender tube up to 15 cm (6 in) long and accompanied by the leaves. It likes a warm sunny place but is easy to grow and increases into clumps. There is a most attractive white form, 'Mani White'. Greece.

C. hadriaticus

A lovely white crocus, usually with a yellow centre and three very conspicuous scarlet stigmas in the middle, identifying it as one of the Saffron crocuses and needing plenty of sun. A soft lilac form is sold as 'Lilacinus'. Greece.

C. kotschyanus (C. zonatus)

This is one of the earliest crocuses to appear in autumn, leafless at flowering time. The stocky goblet-shaped flowers are pale lavender-blue marked with yellow blotches in the centre. 'Albus' is a white-flowered selection and 'Leucopharynx' has a contrasting white throat. Turkey, Syria, Lebanon.

C. laevigatus

This is also described in the winter section, on page 107, since some forms of it flower much later than others. However, it can be in flower from mid-autumn onwards and its colour is very variable, so it is worth trying different forms. The smallish flowers are accompanied by the leaves and have a white or lilac ground colour, variously striped or suffused purple on the outside, sometimes with a biscuit-gold overlay. *C. boryi* is similar but usually has larger, creamy-white flowers with a deep-yellow zone in the throat and a mass of conspicuous orange stigmas. Greece, Crete.

C. medius

A colourful species with rich purple flowers produced before the leaves, much enhanced by the contrasting mass of brilliant orange stigmas in the centre. Best in a hot sunny position. Italy.

C. niveus

One of the largest of the autumn crocuses, with stout-tubed white or pale lavender, yellow-throated flowers, which stand up well to inclement weather. The leaves are produced with the flowers. Greece.

C. nudiflorus

This is excellent for growing in grass, since it enjoys slightly damper conditions than most, and produces stolons that can eventually result in sizeable patches. Its elegant, slender, long-tubed flowers are produced before the leaves, so the grass counteracts its naked apperance. The colour is a rich clear purple but there is also a rare white form. France, Spain.

C. ochroleucus

A smallish late-autumn crocus that will grow in open beds or in grass. Some people find that it increases by offsets so rapidly that they regard it as a pest, but its white, deep-yellow-throated flowers are very welcome at this time of year. It has short stubby leaves at flowering time. Lebanon.

C. pulchellus

One of my favourite crocuses, with very stylish goblet-shaped flowers of a pale clear blue, delicately lined darker, produced before the leaves. There is a rich yellow zone in the centre and orange stigmas, contrasting with the white stamens. It is very easy to cultivate in the open border or in grass. Greece, Turkey.

C. sativus

This, the Saffron crocus, is one of the most handsome of all, with huge, wide-open

flowers of a rich purple, strongly veined and stained darker purple in the centre, produced with the leaves in mid autumn. Saffron is obtained from the three long, deep-red stigma branches, which are plucked and dried – many thousands of flowers being required to make even a small quantity of the well-known colouring/flavouring agent. As a garden plant it is often shy-flowering, but does quite well after hot summers, given a sunny site and rich soil that dries out in summer. Plant the corms at least 10–15 cm (4–6 in) deep or they tend to split up into many small non-flowering ones. It is known only as a cultivated plant, but is probably derived from the Greek species *C. cartwrightianus*. The latter flowers more freely than the Saffron crocus and is a good garden plant for a well-drained sunny position. It has a lovely white form, 'Albus', which retains the scarlet stigmas.

C. serotinus

A very variable crocus, usually flowering at the same time as its leaves, having funnel-shaped flowers in shades of lilac-violet, with

or without a yellow throat. It is an easy and free-flowering species, increasing to form clumps. The most commonly available variant is subsp. *salzmannii* (syn. *C. asturicus*), but the similar subsp. *clusii* is also offered from time to time. Spain, Portugal, North Africa.

C. speciosus

The 'showy crocus' is by far the most frequently seen of all the autumnal species in gardens and should be planted in quantity to produce the best effect. It flowers before the leaves, with large goblet-shaped flowers in pale lilac-blue to deep violet-blue, with an intricate pattern of darker veins and many striking orange stigmas in the centre. The flowers are tall and tend to fall over in bad weather, so it is worth growing them through carpeting plants, or in grass. It is a vigorous species, increasing well by offsets and by seed. The named forms include 'Conqueror', deep blue; 'Globosus', with rounded, bright blue goblet-shaped flowers; 'Oxonian', very deep violet-blue; and 'Albus', the lovely white version. The pale silvery-blue 'Zephyr' is a hybrid with *C. pulchellus*. Greece, western Asia.

C. tournefortii

An unusual crocus in that its pale blue flowers remain widely open in dull weather, even at night, displaying a fountain of orange stigmas and white stamens. The leaves accompany the flowers, so this is a neat plant, well worth growing in an open sunny site with sharp drainage, accompanying small rock plants. Greek islands.

Left: *Cyclamen hederifolium* **is the best and hardiest species for outdoor cultivation and will grow in very dry situations. This seeding colony is in the National Trust garden of Knightshayes Court in Devonshire, England.**

Opposite: The white form of *Crocus speciosus* **growing through a carpet of** *Antennaria dioica.*

Cyclamen

Although *Cyclamen* belong to the same family as the primula and polyanthus, they are very distinct in appearance, since their five petals are sharply reflexed and their rootstocks consist of swollen tubers, so for horticultural purposes they tend to be grouped with bulbs. They are most well known as pot plants in a wide range of flower sizes and colours, all selected from the winter-flowering *C. persicum*; being frost-tender, these are normally cultivated as house or conservatory plants. The wild species (about twenty in all) come mostly from the Mediterranean region, and flower in late summer, autumn, winter and spring, so there are few months when there is not a cyclamen in flower. They are sold as dried tubers in autumn, without leaves or flowers, or as growing plants in pots, and the latter is by far the best way to obtain them, since they give more reliable results.

The autumn-flowering species are delightful for growing in dryish situations where they will receive plenty of sunshine, although the dappled shade of deciduous trees and shrubs is quite acceptable. The soil should be well-drained with a good humus content, preferably as leafmould rather than acid peat. The most frequently cultivated species, *C. hederifolium*, is well worth trying in those 'difficult' situations under pines and other evergreens, since it is very drought-tolerant, provided that it gets just enough moisture in winter to allow the leaves to develop properly. Cyclamen tubers are best planted fairly shallowly, just covered with loose leafy soil and top-dressed each year to prevent them becoming exposed and vulnerable to sun scorch in summer and frost in winter. Most of them grow to 5–10 cm (2–4 in) tall.

Associations: The attractive marbled winter-spring foliage of the hardy cyclamen makes them ideal companions for small spring-flowering bulbs such as snowdrops and winter aconites. It is also worth trying *C. hederifolium* in the cracks of a dry-stone wall, but the tubers are most easily planted when the wall is being built. For underplanting trees and shrubs, they need to be planted in quantity as a drift to be really effective.

C. cilicium

This has small pink or white flowers, usually with a darker purple-red blotch at the base of each petal, although there is also a lovely pure-white form without the blotch. The heart-shaped to rounded leaves have variable silvery patterns on the surface. Turkey.

C. graecum

Although the flowers of this are very similar to the more familiar *C. hederifolium*, the leaves are very different, heart-shaped and with a satin-like surface overlying the very variable pale green or silvery zones, sometimes almost wholly silvery. The flowers may be pale to deep carmine-pink with a darker stain around the mouth, and a pure white form also exists; they are produced just before or with the leaves. This needs a warm sunny position in a gravelly or stony soil, or a rock crevice. Greece, Turkey, eastern Mediterranean islands.

C. hederifolium (C. neapolitanum)

It is true that this, the ivy-leafed cyclamen, does often have leaves that are somewhat ivy-shaped, but they are extremely variable and people have selected a wide range of different shapes, sometimes so long, narrow and pointed that they are lance-shaped. They are also variable in their patterned zones, and sometimes wholly silver. The flowers appear before or with the leaves and range from white ('Album') to deep carmine-pink, scented or unscented. Among the wild cyclamen, this is by far the most accommodating as a garden plant and will seed itself around in a wide variety of soils and situations. Italy to Turkey.

C. mirabile

This is very similar in overall appearance to *C. cilicium*. It has heart-shaped leaves marked with light and dark patterns on the upper side, and they often have a strong purplish-pink staining on the underside and sometimes also on the upper surface. The pale pink flowers have a darker staining at the mouth and the petals are toothed at the tips. South-west Turkey.

It is worth having the autumn snowdrop, *Galanthus reginae-* *olgae*, if only to amaze the neighbours!

C. purpurascens (C. europaeum)

For fragrance, this is the best cyclamen of all, but its pale to deep reddish-purple flowers are produced over a long season from summer to late autumn, rather than all together in a shorter, showier display. The leaves are rounded, usually with silver patterns but sometimes plain green, and are normally present throughout the year. Central and eastern European mountains.

Galanthus (Snowdrop)

Although we do not associate snowdrops with the autumn, there are such things, but only one of them, *G. reginae-olgae*, is at all well known and even that is scarce in gardens. It is, however, well worth obtaining, if only to impress the neighbours! In spite of its rarity, it is not difficult to cultivate and will grow in ordinary neutral to alkaline soil that dries out but is not too hot and sun-baked in summer. It is best to choose a position near deciduous shrubs, which will allow sun through in the autumn and winter but provide a little shade in summer. Planting is best done in spring just before the leaves die down, and most nurseries offering

unusual snowdrops will provide them at this time.

Associations: One of the best plantings I have achieved was a small patch of *G. reginae-olgae* alongside some moss-covered rocks and surrounded by fallen russet-brown leaves, a combination not always easy to arrange!

G. reginae-olgae

The most obvious difference in appearance between this and the ordinary spring snowdrop *G. nivalis*, apart from its flowering time, is that the leaves are dull green with a pale greyish-white stripe along the centre, and they appear just after the flowers. It reaches about 10 cm (4 in) in height. In order to get the autumn-flowering version, one must specify subsp. *reginae-olgae*, since there is also a later-flowering variant, subsp. *vernalis*. Greece.

Leucojum (Snowflake)

The snowflakes are clearly related to the snowdrops, but their flowers have six equal petals rather than three small inner and three large outer ones. Although the autumnal species *L. autumnale* looks very delicate, it is hardier than one might imagine and will grow quite well in an open sunny, but sheltered, situation. The preferred soil appears to be a well-drained, rather sandy one and, when given the right conditions, it will sometimes increase to form quite large grassy clumps. The bulbs are planted as soon as they can be obtained, in the late summer or early autumn, since this is one of the earliest of all the autumn bulbs to flower.

Associations: This charming little plant is too small and elegant to stand much competition from other more colourful plants, but it does look excellent when grown with the smaller ornamental grasses such as *Festuca glauca* and *Stipa tenuifolia*.

L. autumnale

Unlike the spring snowflakes, this has thread-like leaves only 1 mm (⅟₂₅ in) wide, preceded by slender stems up to 15 cm (6 in) tall, each carrying an umbel of up to four small white pendent bells 1–1.5 cm (½–⅝ in) long. *L. roseum* is even smaller, with pale pink bells, and is really so delicate that it is best kept under glass, where its undoubted beauty can be appreciated close at hand. The former is from south-west Europe and North Africa, the latter from Corsica and Sardinia.

Lycoris

These might be considered to be the nerines of Asia, they are so similar in outward appearance, and they are just as beautiful and are hardier but, on the down side, tend to be rather shy-flowering in the cooler-summer areas. Like nerines, they flower before the leaves and have bare stems 30–60 cm (1–2 ft) tall carrying umbels of wavy-petalled flowers; but their colour range is greater, in shades of pink, blue, red, yellow and white. Following the flowers there are strap-like leaves, often grey-green, in some species not appearing until spring. A few species are cultivated quite widely, but this is clearly a genus that has the potential to provide us with a new

range of excellent autumn-flowering bulbs. At present it appears that they do best in areas with hot but not especially dry summers, and there are records of good flowering in the more southerly United States, Japan, Australia and New Zealand. In Europe they seem to be hardy but require a really hot sunny position or glasshouse cultivation to provide the necessary summer heat to encourage flower bud formation. An alkaline soil also seems to be preferred.

Associations: The only successful outdoor plantings in my garden have been in a raised gritty-sandy bed alongside a glasshouse, together with sun-loving lavenders and helichrysums. The scarlet flowers of *L. radiata* looked very attractive indeed with these grey companions.

L. albiflora

A lovely white-flowered species with very undulate, sometimes pinkish-tinted petals and long-protruding stamens. China.

L. aurea

The golden spider lily is aptly named, with beautiful spidery, wavy-petalled flowers in rich yellow-orange. China, Japan.

L. radiata

A bright red-flowered species with narrow, recurving, wavy petals and long-protruding stamens. This has fared better than most *Lycoris* outdoors in my garden. China, Japan.

L. squamigera

One of the better-known and more successful *Lycoris* outdoors, looking rather different from most, since the flowers do not have wavy petals, but are larger and funnel-shaped, more like those of *Amaryllis belladonna*. They are pale rose-purple with a yellow throat. *L. sprengeri* is similar but has flowers of a curious bluish and purple mixture. Both China.

Nerine

Although this is quite a large genus of beautiful autumn-flowering bulbs, only one, *N. bowdenii*, can be regarded as frost-hardy, the rest being plants for growing in a frost-free glasshouse or conservatory as pot plants, and excellent they are for that purpose. They are practically all pink-flowered, but a few

The nerine-like Chinese Lycoris need a summer baking if they are to flower well.

Here, *L. radiata* is growing with colchicums and a seed head of *Allium schubertii*.

are red, and there are albino forms of some. They nearly all have narrow petals, which are very undulate or crisped at the edges, and long-protruding stamens. So there is a distinctive 'nerine appearance', but they range in stature from robust plants up to 70 cm (2⅓ ft) in height with strap-shaped foliage to tiny species only 15 cm (6 in) tall with thread-like leaves. Apart from the wild species there are many hybrids and selections with brilliantly coloured flowers in a range of hues, mostly in red/salmon/pink shades, but these are all tender plants.

The hardy *N. bowdenii* and its colour forms can easily be grown anywhere there is a warm sunny position sheltered from the worst of the ground-freezing frosts. In bad winters the leaves are often damaged but the plants usually recover from this. The bulbs can be planted in early autumn or in spring but, if the latter, they should be watered sparingly throughout the summer to encourage the formation of new roots. Although it is often said that they need to be near the surface, in cold areas they should be just covered with soil to protect them a little from the frost. On the whole they are best left undisturbed for as long as the clumps are growing and flowering well, but if they become too congested and flowering ceases, it is best to lift them and tease out the bulbs individually and then replant

them, spaced out a little. Before lifting shy-flowering clumps it is worth trying regular feeds throughout the autumn – spring growing season of a potash-rich (tomato) fertilizer. During summer, when they are resting, it is important that the soil where the bulbs are growing receives plenty of warm sun to encourage flower buds for the coming season.

Associations: The icing-sugar-pink flowers of nerines associate well with both grey-leaved and purple-leaved plants, so it is worth experimenting with various combinations, such as the purple-leaved sage *Salvia officinalis* 'Purpurea' and some of the euphorbias like *E. wulfenii*, but take care to plant these so that they do not shade the nerines in summer.

Top: Nerine bowdenii is the hardiest of the Cape nerines, requiring a warm sunny position for its summer-dormant bulbs to form flower buds for the coming autumn.

Bottom: Sternbergia lutea is a sun-loving Mediterranean plant, crocus-like but related to the daffodil.

N. bowdenii

After a summer rest, this will produce stout 45–70 cm (18 in–2⅓ ft) stems, each with an umbel of several sparkling pink wavy-petalled flowers. The strap-like leaves appear later and last throughout the winter until the following early summer. The normal form is a superb plant, but for enthusiasts there are other varieties, including 'Pink Triumph', which has richer pink flowers, and 'Mark Fenwick', a taller, vigorous plant with more, darker-pink flowers in each umbel. South Africa.

N. sarniensis (Guernsey Lily)

This is less hardy than *N. bowdenii* but, in very mild gardens, it may be worth trying it against a warm wall of the house. It has very striking intensely red flowers, several in dense umbels on 45–60 cm (18 in–2 ft) stems. The English name apparently derives from the fact that some bulbs, bound for Holland on a ship that ran aground on Guernsey, were given to locals who assisted in the rescue of the grateful crew, but it actually originates from South Africa.

Sternbergia

Although these are members of the amaryllis family, and are therefore related to the daffodil, their flowers are wineglass-shaped and look much more like large yellow crocuses. The bulbs are, however, very daffodil-like, and produce fleshy strap-like leaves together with the flowers in the autumn after a summer rest period, or, in some species, after the flowers have finished. The best species for garden display are *S. lutea* and *S. sicula*, which require sunny situations where the bulbs get warmed during the summer months, encouraging flower buds to form within the dormant bulbs, ready for the coming flowering season. Although I have seen good flowering clumps on acid sandy formations, they appear to do best on heavier alkaline soils, provided that the bulbs dry out to some extent in summer. They are normally planted in late summer or early autumn, but established clumps can be lifted, divided and replanted satisfactorily in late spring while the leaves are still green.

Associations: One of the best plantings of *S. lutea* I have seen was at the base of a yew hedge where the bulbs must get extremely warm and dry in summer. The combination of the brilliant golden blooms with the deep green of the yew was stunning when there was a good flowering season. They look best, of course, when seen among the roots of an olive tree or amid rocks in their native Mediterranean!

S. lutea

At one time this was freely available from nurseries, but it has become less common in recent years. It is certainly the showiest, with large bright yellow goblet-shaped flowers, one per stem, about 3–5.5 cm (1¼–2¼ in) long and accompanied by glossy green strap-like leaves. The whole plant when in flower is no more than about 15 cm (6 in) tall. Mediterranean region.

S. sicula

Very similar to *S. lutea* but generally an altogether more compact plant, 8–10 cm (3⅛–4 in) in height with smaller flowers up

to 3.5 cm (1⅜ in) long, although large for the size of the plant, with narrower dark green leaves, which often have a conspicuous whitish stripe along the centre of the upper surface. I find that this flowers much more freely than *S. lutea* in the open garden and increases well. Italy, Greece, Turkey.

Zephyranthes (Rain Lily)

These are rather comparable with sternbergias, in that they belong to the amaryllis family and are rather like large autumn crocuses in their flower shape. They do best if given a position where they will be hot and comparatively dry during the summer when at rest. Unfortunately, only one species, *Z. candida*, is reliably frost-hardy, which is a great pity as there is a vast

range of species and they are relatively easy to cultivate, although their display is short-lived. The bulbs are usually offered for planting in spring and should be kept watered for the first season to encourage root formation. They may not flower well in the autumn after planting and are best left undisturbed to increase into clumps over a period of years; only lift and split them if flowering begins to decline.

Associations: Like the sternbergias, these are best in warm sheltered borders without too much competition, which might shade them and prevent flower bud formation; however, they do look better if accompanied by other plants. Suitable companions requiring a similar site are the various forms of *Iris unguicularis*, the winter Algerian iris, which will flower later on in winter, thus prolonging the season of interest.

Z. candida

This carries large, single crocus-shaped white flowers about 3.5 cm (1⅜ in) long, facing upwards on stems about 15–20 cm (6–8 in) in height, accompanied by erect rush-like green leaves. Argentina, Uruguay.

Z. grandiflora

As with *Z. candida*, this might be worth trying in very mild areas. It has striking bright pink, widely funnel-shaped flowers 7–8 cm (2¾–3⅛ in) long. Central America.

The South American *Zephyranthes* are mostly not frost-hardy but *Z. candida* can be grown in quite cold areas if planted by a warm wall.

The winter garden need not be dull. Here *Cyclamen coum*, snowdrops and winter aconites provide a long-lasting and welcome winter break.

THE FINAL FLING:
BULBS IN BLEAK MIDWINTER

In some ways, of course, winter is a most enjoyable season, since the few plants that are in flower at this time are probably appreciated individually far more than those that flower along with hundreds of other plants during the summer.

There are really two ways of using winter-flowering bulbs: they can be dotted around the garden to spread the interest over a wide area, livening up otherwise dull spots; or they can be grouped together in an 'all eggs in one basket' approach, to provide as stunning a show as possible in one area. Both ways can be successful, and there is no reason why both should not be incorporated into planting plans, but there are a few hints that may be helpful when trying to decide how best to make use of these rather precious winter blooms.

The few winter-flowering shrubs such as the viburnums, winter jasmine and witch hazel can be much enhanced if accompanied by underplantings of bulbs, and those with colourful twigs can also be combined extremely successfully with early bulbs, while associations of winter heathers with

The ornamental winter leaves of *Arum italicum* 'Marmoratum' are an excellent accompaniment for other early bulbs.

crocuses, snowdrops and winter aconites are delightful. It is well worth siting these plantings so that they are visible from the main rooms of the house.

BULBS FOR THE WINTER

Arum

These fascinating plants, the Lords and Ladies or Cuckoo Pints, are not normally associated with winter, but a few do produce their attractive arrow-shaped leaves in the autumn and last throughout the winter into spring. Some forms of *A. italicum* are so ornamental that they have become popular foliage plants, both in the garden and in flower arrangements. The sail- or cowl-like spathes are mostly produced in spring, followed by clusters of red berries in autumn. Arum tubers are planted in autumn in a semi-shaded or sunny position in any ordinary garden soil, provided it is not waterlogged.

Associations: Try a combined planting of *A. italicum*, for its foil of attractive leaves, with snowdrops, hellebores and winter aconites, in dappled shade.

A. italicum

This has the best foliage, some forms being marked with creamy veins, others variegated more conspicuously with silvery cream. 'Marmoratum' ('Pictum') is the most commonly available cultivar, with extremely frost-hardy arrow-shaped leaves that are 12–20 cm (4¾–8 in) long. The creamy or pale green spathes appear in late spring. Mediterranean region.

Crocus

Although few crocuses are naturally winter-flowering, the many cultivars and hybrids of *C. chrysanthus* often open their first blooms as soon as the days begin to lengthen, and *C. tommasinianus* is one of the earliest of all the hardy bulbs to appear. The only commercially available one that can be said to be truly winter-flowering is *C. laevigatus*, which will flower at any time from late autumn to late winter, pushing up buds whenever there is a break in the weather. Most crocuses need a sunny position in well-drained soil, but *C. tommasinianus* will take dappled shade and will seed itself around naturally when well suited. They all reach heights of 5–10 cm (2–4 in).

Right top: *Crocus tommasinianus* is one of the best for naturalizing, seeding freely; it will grow through later-flowering carpeting alpines.
Bottom: The Greek *Crocus laevigatus* blooms in the depths of winter, so needs a sheltered position.

Left top: The many cultivars of *Crocus chrysanthus* and *C. biflorus* flower at the first hint of spring.
Bottom: *Crocus tommasinianus* and *Helleborus foetidus* in the winter garden at the National Trust's garden of Polesden Lacey in Surrey, England.

Associations: For a planting of *C. laevigatus* choose a protected site, for example on the sheltered side of a small evergreen shrub – silvery conifers make suitable backgrounds – or among perennial ornamental grasses. Make sure that the position is one that catches all the available winter sunshine, or the flowers will not open properly. The *C. tommasinianus* varieties are worth planting in the sunny parts of shrub borders where they can be left undisturbed to naturalize. For a cheerful late-winter scene, a delightful combination is *C. tommasinianus* with snowdrops and the coloured twigs of coppiced *Salix alba* var. *vitellina* and *Cornus alba* 'Sibirica'.

C. chrysanthus

This will be found, together with its relative *C. biflorus*, in the spring selection on page 34.

C. laevigatus

A delightful crocus in variable shades of lilac-blue or white, usually with darker purple veins on the outside and beautifully scented. A good midwinter variant is 'Fontenayi', in which the fairly large lilac flowers are conspicuously striped dark purple. Greece, Crete.

C. tommasinianus

Although some people complain about the freedom with which this bright little crocus seeds itself around in gardens, it is really almost indispensable, since it bursts into flower as soon as there is a hint of warmth in the late winter sunshine and comes in a great range of variants. The slender flowers open to a starry shape, normally pale lavender with a silvery wash outside, but there are darker forms such as 'Barr's Purple', 'Whitewell Purple', 'Ruby Giant'

and a good white, 'Eric Smith'. However, when these are grown together many others will arise – some pinkish, some with dark tips, and others with whitish tips. Montenegro.

Cyclamen

As with crocuses, there is only one reliably hardy winter-flowering cyclamen, *C. coum*, but it is a most valuable and extremely variable species, so it is possible to have many different-looking plants. *C. persicum* must also be mentioned, since it is a very familiar plant and is naturally winter-flowering; unfortunately it is not hardy and in cold areas is best grown in a cool conservatory. The wild form is slightly hardier than the large-flowered selections, and it might be possible to grow it in sheltered areas where there is little frost.

Cyclamen require an open soil, lightened with a little well-rotted organic matter. In the case of the hardy species, they can be planted or moved in the autumn just before growth commences, or at almost any time if bought as potted plants. The tubers should be covered by only 2–3 cm (¾–1¼ in) of loose soil or composted bark chips.

Associations: *C. coum* looks very attractive planted among winter heathers, *Erica carnea*, and these, being evergreens, afford it some protection. Diverse combinations can be tried using the different colour forms of the cyclamen with various heather cultivars.

C. coum

This is very variable, the rounded or heart-shaped leaves being up to 8 cm (3⅛ in) long and ranging from plain dark green to silver-zoned in varying degrees, through to almost wholly silver or pewter-coloured. The flowers are small, only 8–15 mm (⅓–⅝ in) long, but come in many bright shades of purplish-magenta with an even darker patch at the 'nose' of the flower, and there are also white forms. So by combining the leaf and flower colour variations there are almost endless possibilities, and all are attractive. Some of the excellent named cultivars include: 'Nymans', deep magenta; 'Tilebarn Elizabeth', bicoloured shading from a white centre to rose at the petal edges; 'Album', with white flowers and plain green leaves; and 'Maurice Dryden', white-flowered with beautifully silvered leaves. The silvery-leaved forms are sometimes merged as the 'Pewter Group'. Widespread in western Asia.

C. persicum

This is the species from which all the florists' pot-plant cyclamen have been derived by a process of selection. It varies a great deal in flower colour and size, and in the pale or silver patterns on the leaves. The elegant, long-petalled, deliciously fragrant flowers of the wild forms may be white to deep carmine-red with a darker 'nose'. Many named cultivar groups are now available, some fairly dwarf and resembling the wild forms, which have been given descriptive names such as 'Dwarf Scented', through to the very large florists' forms, which show a wide array of colours and sometimes have their petals

prominently fringed; even a yellow form has been selected, a colour quite unknown in the wild. *C. persicum* is among our most popular pot plants for the winter months, although they rarely last long as house plants, since they cannot tolerate the heat and are much better in a cool room or conservatory at not more than about 10°C (50°F). Eastern Mediterranean.

Eranthis

The winter aconite is usually true to its name in my garden, although in a bad winter it may well wait until the first hint of spring before opening its yellow cups. This is naturally a woodland plant, so it is best to find a spot where it will not become too hot and dry in summer. When happy, it will seed itself around and form carpets beneath deciduous trees and shrubs.

Associations: There is no better sight in the late winter than winter aconites accompanying the first of the hellebores – which are botanical and geographical allies – in the dappled shade of trees, together with snowdrops. Clumps of aconites amid winter heathers can also be very effective and successful.

Top: The winter-flowering *Cyclamen coum* naturalized in Washington State in the Kirkland garden of the late Brian Mulligan and his wife Margaret. Bottom: The flowers of *Cyclamen coum* are very frost-resistant. There are many selections with varying flower colours and leaf patterns.

Opposite: The very fragrant *Cyclamen persicum* is not frost-hardy but is a superb winter-flowering bulb for mild areas or a conservatory.

E. cilicica

Although less easy to obtain, this is well worth seeking; it has similar flowers to *E. hyemalis* but they are a deeper shade of yellow and the leaves are of a rich bronzy green when they first unfurl. It prefers a slightly more open situation than *E. hyemalis*. Turkey.

E. hyemalis (Winter Aconite)

This familiar little plant has a solitary upright yellow flower about 3 cm (1¼ in) across, which sits, stemless, on a ruff of deeply cut 'leaves', the whole thing carried on a short stalk up to about 10 cm (4 in) above the ground. It is ideal ground cover, except for the fact that it disappears almost as quickly as it arrives. The 'standard' form is delightful, but there are also rare sought-after selections with coppery and creamy-coloured flowers. Europe.

E. × tubergenii

When the above two hybridize they produce striking seedlings with larger flowers. Like *E. cilicica*, they prefer a little more sun than *E. hyemalis*. 'Guinea Gold' is an excellent named selection with large rich golden flowers and bronzy foliage.

Galanthus

The snowdrops are among the best loved of bulbs, instantly recognizable on account of their small pendent white flowers, in which the three outer petals are much larger than the three inner. They can be in flower from autumn to early spring, some of them reliably blooming in the depths of winter. There are a few frequently cultivated

species but, from these, snowdrop fanciers have selected an enormous number of cultivars – single and double – differing slightly in size, leaf colour and shape, and in the extent of the green markings on their petals. They are currently undergoing something of a popularity boom, so that increasing numbers of varieties are becoming available. Snowdrops are marketed either as dormant bulbs in autumn or, more frequently nowadays, as growing plants in spring when in leaf. They can be cultivated in a wide range of soil conditions, provided that it does not become too hot and dusty dry in summer. A heavy alkaline soil seems to suit them

best although, with the addition of plenty of old organic matter, light sandy soils can also give good results. A position in dappled shade is probably ideal for most, but *G. elwesii*, *G. reginae-olgae* and *G. gracilis* do appreciate a little more sun than the common *G. nivalis*. Most of them grow up to 10–15 cm (4–6 in) tall.

Associations: Snowdrops associate well with almost any of the other winter-blooming plants, but look especially appealing when grown under deciduous trees and shrubs accompanying hellebores, winter aconites, *Cyclamen coum* and *Arum italicum* 'Marmoratum'.

G. caucasicus

Although this is a familiar name, most snowdrops under this name in gardens are probably forms of *G. elwesii*.

G. cilicicus

Although very similar in appearance to the common snowdrop, this is regarded as a distinct species. I find that it flowers very early on in midwinter, well before *G. nivalis*, and has narrow, very grey leaves. Turkey.

G. elwesii

Compared with most other species this is a large plant, and is sometimes known as the giant snowdrop. It has broad, conspicuously grey-green leaves up to 30 cm (12 in) long and 3 cm (1¼ in) across, widest near the apex and 'hooded' at the tip. The flowers are variable, usually larger than those of the above (up to 3 cm/ 1¼ in long) and often with two green marks

Left: Some selections of *Galanthus elwesii* flower in the depths of winter.

Opposite top: The winter aconite, *Eranthis hyemalis*, associates well with *Erica carnea*. Bottom: The larger *Eranthis* 'Guinea Gold' will take a little more sun than the winter aconite.

on each inner petal, one at the base and one at the tip, sometimes merging to form a green stripe. In cultivation certain forms have been referred to as '*G. caucasicus*', and some, such as 'Hiemale', are superb winter-flowering plants, carrying on from the autumnal *G. reginae-olgae* into winter. Balkans, western Asia.

G. fosteri
This also has flowers with two green blotches on each inner petal, but is distinctive in having bright green leaves. It is a rather rare plant in gardens and is, I find, not quite as easy to please, probably requiring a slightly sunnier position. Turkey, Lebanon.

G. gracilis
This can be distinguished by its narrow, grey-green leaves, which are twisted lengthways, combined with the fact that the flowers have two green marks on each inner petal, at the base and tip. It seems to prefer slightly more sun than most. Western Turkey, Greece, Bulgaria.

G. ikariae and G. woronowii (G. latifolius)
These two are similar in having wide, bright shiny green leaves. The flowers are rather like those of *G. nivalis*, with green marks only at the tips of the inner petals. Eastern Aegean islands, Turkey, the Caucasus.

G. nivalis
This, the common snowdrop, normally flowers somewhat later than many of the others, although in many gardens it can still be in flower by late winter. The smallish flowers have only one green blotch at the apex of each inner petal and the grey leaves are rather narrow. Selections of it include 'Lutescens', a small form in which the markings are yellow rather than green, and 'Flore Pleno', a double form with many more petals than normal. 'Scharlockii' has two long spathes sticking up like ears above the flowers, and 'Viridapicis' has green tips to the outer petals as well as the inner. Widespread in Europe.

G. plicatus

Most of the variations of this large
snowdrop flower slightly later, in late
winter or early spring. It has broad greyish-
green leaves, which have their margins
turned downwards in a characteristic
manner. The substantial flowers have a
green patch at the apex of each inner
petal, while subsp. *byzantinus* has two
patches, one at the base and one at the
apex. *G. plicatus* has given rise to some
fine vigorous hybrid snowdrops. Crimea,
Bulgaria, Romania, Turkey.

G. rizehensis

A small-flowered, rather dainty species,
with narrow dark green leaves contrasting
with the purity of the flowers; the inner
petals have small green marks at the apex
only. Turkey.

Galanthus cultivars

There are many selections and hybrids
now available, some very fine robust garden
plants, others quirky mutations sought by
enthusiasts and collectors. A few of my
favourites are 'Atkinsii', a very vigorous one,
which has elongate flowers on long stems;
'Sam Arnott', a strong one with heart-
shaped green marks on the inner petals;
'Kite', with robust, broad grey foliage and
long, elegant flowers; 'Magnet', in which
the flowers are held out on a long slender
stalk away from the main stem; 'Augustus',

Galanthus 'Atkinsii'
planted beneath
Viburnum ×
bodnantense **in a**
winter garden display.

a *plicatus* hybrid with very wide, bold, dark
green leaves dusted with a grey 'bloom';
and 'Poculiformis', which has a very
distinctive appearance, since the six petals
are all the same size and unmarked with
green. 'Merlin' has its inner petals almost
wholly stained with green, while 'Straffan'
is notable for its large solid-textured flowers
marked with horseshoe green marks on the
inner petals. Although some people dislike
doubles, since their many petals obscure the
elegant, classical snowdrop shape, there are
some large and very striking ones,
including 'Lady Beatrix Stanley',
'Hippolyta' and 'Dionysus'.

Iris

The main group of irises for flowering in
winter and early spring is the Reticulata
group (subgenus Hermodactyloides). The
very popular and attractive *I. reticulata*,
and all its many colour selections and
hybrids, could be regarded as spring-
flowering, although in mild winters they
are sometimes in flower as early as the
related *I. histrioides*, which is described
below. The same applies to the yellow
I. danfordiae, which will be found, together
with *I. reticulata*, in the spring section on
page 46. Although rhizomatous rather than
bulbous, one must not forget the Algerian
iris, *I. unguicularis*, which is a superb
winter-flowering plant.

Associations: The small bulbous irises can
be grown to great effect in a gravelly bed
amid grey-leaved plants, which act as an
attractive background for the blue flowers –
for example, amid some of the smaller
Dianthus, which will flower later on after
the irises have finished. *I. unguicularis*
can also be accompanied to great effect
by grey-leaved sun-loving shrubs such as
Convolvulus cneorum and *Cistus* species, as
long as the shrubs do not grow over the
irises and shade them.

I. histrioides

This is a very attractive species, which
does extremely well in the open ground,
increasing into clumps unless it is attacked
by 'ink disease', which can wipe out patches
in one season. The large, stocky, deep-blue
flowers, which are about 6–7 cm (2½–2¾ in)
across, emerge in mid to late winter almost

before the leaves begin to show, and are extremely frost-hardy, recovering without blemish even when they have been frozen stiff. For some unaccountable reason, *I. histrioides* has become scarce in recent years but is now beginning to reappear in catalogues. The colour varies a little, in shades of rich violet-blue, blotched darker in the centre of the three larger outer petals, where there is also an orange splash. Some of the variations have been named, for example 'Lady Beatrix Stanley' and 'Major', but all are equally worth having. My best plants grow in full sun in a raised bed of gritty-sandy soil. I should mention also the similar *I. histrio*, which is, on the whole, paler blue in colour with more prominent blotching on the petals, and has quite extensive foliage at flowering time. This starts to flower earlier and is much less tolerant of cold winters, so it is really a plant for the unheated glasshouse. The smaller-flowered *I. histrio* subsp. *aintabensis* is hardier and is more successful outside. *I. histrioides* and *I. histrio* are from Turkey, the latter extending to Lebanon.

I. unguicularis

Although I have, in general, not included rhizomatous plants in this book, I have slipped in the winter-flowering Algerian iris, since there is a dearth of flowers at this time of year and it is such a valuable plant for this purpose. It is an evergreen, and requires protection for its leaves and fragile long-tubed blooms, which can start to appear at any time from late autumn right through to early spring. The rhizomes also need to be well ripened during the summer rest period if they are to flower freely, so

this is a plant that appreciates a warm sunny position. In Britain it is often planted against a sunny wall for extra warmth and protection. The flower colour varies from pale lavender, like 'Walter Butt', to deep purple, as in 'Mary Barnard', or white in the case of 'Alba'. The long-tubed flowers are 10–15 cm (4–6 in) high, but the foliage reaches 45 cm (18 in). Mediterranean region.

Narcissus

Although we naturally associate daffodils with the spring, since that is when most of them make their display, there are a few that can be regarded as winter-flowering, and some are even autumnal. Naturally, any narcissus flowering at this potentially

inclement time of year is liable to damage by wind, rain and frost, but it is well worth taking the chance and planting a few, since it is surprising just how resilient some of them are, in spite of their delicate appearance. The early varieties of the larger trumpet daffodils can be planted out in the open border among other perennials, preferably protected from the worst of the winter winds, but the smaller species and hybrids need a well-drained sunny, sheltered position if they are to thrive. They are very suitable for a raised bed, where they can be seen more closely.

Associations: The yellow trumpet daffodils always tend to look best in grass, since that is their natural habitat and the flowers stand out better, but groups planted among dark-leaved evergreen shrubs such as rhododendrons brighten an otherwise dull scene early in the year, and are given some welcome protection by them. The small early *Narcissus* species need a warm sunny spot and look well when flowering with other small bulbs requiring similar conditions, such as *Iris histrioides* and *I. reticulata*. I grow these in a raised gritty-sandy bed with small alpines, particularly those with silvery leaves.

The Algerian iris, *Iris unguicularis*, is a good winter-flowering 'bulb' for a hot sunny position; there are many colour forms.

**Right: Forms of
Narcissus bulbocodium
and other hoop
petticoat daffodils
start to flower in
early winter and carry
through to spring;
these later-flowering
ones are combined
with dog's tooth
violets in grass.**

**Opposite: Although
in appearance an
ordinary trumpet
daffodil, 'Rijnveld's
Early Sensation'
flowers long before
most of the others.**

N. bulbocodium (Hoop Petticoat Daffodil)
Although this could be included with the
spring-flowering bulbs, I am describing
it here since it will then accompany its
relatives below, *N. cantabricus* and
N. romieuxii, and I do actually have a
small clump of one form that has been in
flower out in the garden since just after
Christmas – our mid-winter, for those
who might be reading this in the Southern
Hemisphere! *N. bulbocodium*, in all its
multitude of variations, is a superb plant,
which will charm anyone who is lucky
enough to see the drifts of it growing in the
grassy meadows at the Royal Horticultural
Society's gardens at Wisley and the Savill
Gardens at Windsor. The stocky, rich
yellow flowers on 10–20 cm (4–8 in)
stems, with their wide funnel-shaped cup

surrounded by six narrow petals, give the
hoop petticoat daffodil and its relatives
a distinctive appearance. But, within this
overall shape, there are many possibilities
for variation, and avid collectors can
acquire numerous forms, for example
var. *conspicuus*, var. *nivalis*, var. *citrinus*,
subsp. *praecox* and subsp. *obesus*. Since each
of these in itself varies, there are almost
endless possibilities. Suffice to say that they
are all delightful, so obtain as few or as
many as you like, try them in different
situations in the garden and enjoy the
results, if the experimentation is successful!
N. bulbocodium is a native of south-west
Europe and North Africa.

N. cantabricus
From the point of view of garden value,
this may be regarded as a white hoop
petticoat daffodil, but it and its many
variations are very special and much sought
after by bulb and alpine plant enthusiasts.
It is extremely variable and there are several
named forms, such as subsp. *monophyllus*,
subsp. *tananicus*, var. *foliosus* and var.
petunioides, but it must be said that all are
attractive and, unless one is making a study
or a collection of them, any will do. The
last of these is perhaps the most desirable,
having a very widely flaring cup with a
frilly edge. There are others as well, and a
search through specialist literature and bulb
catalogues will reveal more, although there
is considerable confusion and no guarantee
of uniformity within any particular name!

For most gardeners in colder areas these are not really plants for outdoors, although it is always worth a try when enough bulbs have been propagated so that a few casualties do not matter; these fragile-looking plants are often tougher than they appear, being, for the most part, mountain plants in the wild. They grow up to 8–12 cm (3⅛–4¾ in) tall. I should also mention a group of variable hybrids known collectively as *N.* 'Nylon', which are derived from *N. cantabricus* and *N. romieuxii*, having cream to pale sulphur-coloured flowers. These were in flower in my garden in the depths of winter and have continued to bloom quite undaunted by wind, rain, on-and-off snow cover and fluctuating temperatures down to −9°C (13°F). *N. cantabricus* is a native of North Africa and southern Spain.

N. hedraeanthus

This diminutive hoop petticoat daffodil, just 5–7 cm (2–2¾ in) tall, has flowers so small that it is really not worth planting it outside – it needs to be raised up in a pot on a bench, where it can be seen. It is, however, hardy and will grow outside, and can flower very early, so if the right spot can be found on a raised bed it is worth trying. The very small, pale greenish-yellow flowers are held just above the ground amid coiled wiry leaves and tend to face obliquely upwards or even almost vertically, with protruding stamens. Spain.

N. romieuxii

An extremely variable and apparently delicate little species, but the flowers are actually quite weather-resistant, although the slugs love them and need to be dealt

with ruthlessly! It is only 10–15 cm (4–6 in) in height, with wiry thread-like leaves, and has the typical 'hoop petticoat' flower with narrow petals and a wide funnel-shaped cup in variable shades of sulphur-yellow. These can be produced at any time from early winter through to spring, depending upon the locality of the garden and the mildness of the season. In cold areas it may be better to try it in pots in an unheated cold or frost-free greenhouse where the delicate blooms can be enjoyed at eye level. A sharply drained sandy soil mix suits it well, so that the bulbs dry out somewhat during their summer rest period. As with its relatives *N. bulbocodium* and *N. cantabricus*, there are several named variants, one of which, under the name of var. *mesatlanticus*, is very successful in

gardens – a vigorous free-flowering plant with pale greenish-sulphur flowers. Other good forms may be found in specialist collections as subsp. *albidus* and var. *zaianicus*, both of which have whiter flowers, tinged with green or pale yellow. Morocco.

N. 'Cedric Morris'

A splendid small daffodil only 10–15 cm (4–6 in) in height, similar to *N. asturiensis* (see page 51), although the flowers are produced even earlier and are normally well over by the time the more familiar spring daffodils are beginning to show through the ground. Although it was found in the wild in Spain, there is no general agreement as to which species it belongs to, but this just adds to its interest. The small yellow flowers, which have trumpets that are flared and frilled at the mouth, are accompanied by narrow grey leaves. The size dictates that it is only really useful for the front of a border or, even better, a raised bed or rock garden in a sunny well-drained spot.

N. 'Rijnveld's Early Sensation'

Although a fairly ordinary-looking, normal-sized yellow trumpet daffodil, this is much earlier than most of its kind, far ahead of the (in my garden) inaptly named 'February Gold' which, as I write, in February, is currently just pushing through the ground, whereas 'Rijnveld's' is in bud. I have not grown 'Dawn Chorus', but its description makes it sound very similar; it is also regarded as one of the earliest. Garden hybrid.

The Cape romuleas such as *R. tortuosa* are highly colourful and varied compared with the hardier Mediterranean species. Photographed at the University of California Botanic Garden, Irvine.

THE AMAZING CAPE BULBS:
AN INTRODUCTION TO SOUTH AFRICAN BULBS

The south-western part of South Africa – the south-west Cape – has an enormous range of very colourful, exciting bulbs, which are, on the whole, largely unknown to the average gardener and most are, as yet, unobtainable through the nursery trade. However, they are increasing in popularity and I am quite sure that we are at the start of an upsurge of interest in these fascinating bulbs.

One drawback, and this is the main reason they are not known more widely, is that most are not very frost-hardy and, in cold winter regions such as Britain, Europe and a considerable part of North America, they require cultivation under glass, although heat is needed only at the level of frost protection. They are, however, excellent plants for the slightly heated conservatory, since they are generally very easy to cultivate in pots or containers in a sandy potting medium, and are valuable in that they flower in winter or early spring. After they have died down they can be dried off for the summer until re-potting time in early

Hesperantha vaginata **is typical of the showiness of many of the Cape bulbs.**

autumn, so they are really very little trouble, while being extremely rewarding.

In the warmer areas of their native South Africa, Australia, New Zealand and the United States – especially California – many of them can be grown outside without protection, which may appear to be a great advantage, but a few have become notorious weeds outside their native lands. If there is any doubt about a bulb's hardiness or, conversely, whether it might become a pest, it is always worth experimenting by growing it in containers until some experience of its behaviour has been gained.

These south-west Cape bulbs are from a predominantly winter-rainfall area and are therefore in growth throughout the winter months, so the bulbs should be planted in early autumn. However, in the case of a few genera, such as *Ixia*, *Freesia*, *Sparaxis* and *Babiana*, some nurserymen in cold-winter regions – especially in The Netherlands – store them artificially warm and dry during the winter so that they remain dormant, then offer them for sale in the spring catalogues for planting in spring to flower in summer. But it must be remembered that these are naturally winter-growers and they will revert to this habit unless the regime is repeated, lifting the bulbs or corms in autumn and storing them dry until the following spring.

There are hundreds of species of beautiful Cape bulbs and the following list represents just a few that are around in cultivation. The enthusiast will find that many more are cultivated by fellow enthusiasts, or are obtainable through the seed lists of various societies and specialist nurseries.

THE CAPE BULBS

Babiana

Babianas are most likely to be offered as a mixed collection in various colours from pale to deep blue, violet, white or yellow. They are mostly 10–25 cm (4–10 in) tall with hairy leaves, which are ribbed or pleated lengthways, and funnel-shaped flowers in short spikes, somewhat freesia-like. If grown in pots, choose tall ones, since the bulbs like to be deep in the soil, 10–12 cm (4–4¾ in) at least.

B. cedarbergensis – pale blue, fragrant
B. odorata – bright yellow, fragrant
B. pygmaea – bright yellow with a blackish throat
B. rubrocyanea – bright blue with a large red zone in the centre
B. stricta – variable shades of purple-blue
B. villosa – reddish-purple

Chasmanthe

These are large plants 1 m (3¼ ft) or more tall, with erect fans of bold leaves and spikes of orange-red or yellow curved-tubular flowers in late spring or early summer. In mild areas they will form large montbretia-like clumps; otherwise, grow them in large containers.

C. aethiopica – 5 cm (2 in) long orange-red flowers, upper petal hooded
C. floribunda – more robust with larger flowers and wider leaves
C. floribunda var. *duckittii* – yellow-flowered version

Cyanella

Although these are not very showy, they have interesting white, yellow or blue flowers with reflexed petals on loosely branched or unbranched stems; the long narrow leaves are often undulate at the edges.

C. lutea – starry yellow flowers, 20–30 cm (8–12 in) tall
C. orchidiformis – lavender-blue flowers, 15–20 cm (6–8 in) tall

Ferraria

Intriguing plants in the iris family, 15–20 cm (6–8 in) tall, which have flat fans of narrow leaves, often curved like a sickle, and a succession of flattish flowers. These have three large outer petals and three smaller inner ones, usually strongly crisped at the edges. The colours are remarkable, in shades and mixtures of brown, blackish-purple, dusky yellow and blue, often accompanied by an unpleasant smell.

F. crispa – brownish-purple with creamy, dark-blotched centre

Freesia

Few of the wild species in this well-known genus are in general cultivation, most of the popularity being reserved for the many large-flowered hybrids that are frequently cultivated as cut flowers. It is, however, well worth trying some of the species, since they are, although often smaller-flowered, very fragrant. Some nurserymen sell dried corms for planting in spring, but they are naturally winter-growers for planting in the autumn. They grow up to 20–30 cm (8–12 in) tall.

F. alba – fragrant white flowers, flushed purple on lower petals
F. corymbosa – yellow or pink with orange marks on lower petals
F. refracta – greenish-yellow with deeper orange markings
'Romany' – large 'double' pale-purple flowers with extra petals
'Royal Blue' – violet with a white throat, striped darker
'Royal Gold' – buttercup-yellow, edged darker orange
'White Swan' – creamy-white with a yellow throat

Geissorhiza

These are members of the iris family, with starry or funnel-shaped flowers in spikes opening only in bright sunlight, so keep them in as light a position as possible under glass.

G. furva – bright purple-red
G. radians – deep blue with a white circle around the red centre
G. splendidissima – deep rich violet-blue

Gladiolus

The summer-growing gladioli, or their derivatives, are well known world-wide but the colourful, and far more varied and interesting, 'winter-rainfall' species are seldom seen or available from nurseries, in spite of being relatively easy to cultivate, given the frost protection they require.

They are late-winter to mid-spring flowering, unless otherwise noted, and are mostly 15–40 cm (6–16 in) in height in cultivation.

G. alatus – hooded red flowers with yellow and green markings
G. carmineus – pink with white marks on lower petals; autumn
G. carneus – creamy-white with purple splashes on lower petals
G. citrinus – funnel-shaped flowers, golden yellow
G. tristis – pale yellow or creamy-green, very fragrant

Hesperantha

These are very similar to the geissorhizas mentioned above, although often not as brightly coloured and tending to open during the evening. One species is, however, extremely dramatic and well worth growing.

H. vaginata – yellow with black tips and centre

Hessea and Strumaria

Hessea are small members of the Amaryllidaceae, resembling tiny nerines and flowering in autumn soon after growth commences, only 10–15 cm (4–6 in) tall when in flower. They have thread-like to narrowly strap-like leaves and loose umbels of small, usually flat, starry flowers, often with undulate petals. Very similar is *Strumaria*, a few species of which are also cultivated. Although far from showy, these

graceful little plants have a delicate charm and provide interest in the autumn months.

H. zeyheri – small white flowers with narrow, crisped petals
S. rubella – small starry pink flowers, the petals not crisped

Homeria

These are attractive spring-flowering bulbs, often with upright, widely bowl-shaped flowers in attractive pastel colours, but some of them have a tendency to weediness and are poisonous to livestock, so they must be treated with caution in places where they are hardy. In cold-winter areas they seldom survive the winter and are better treated as container plants for a conservatory. They grow 30–45 cm (12–18 in) tall with long narrow leaves and several rounded flowers 5 cm (2 in) in diameter produced in succession.

H. collina – variable in colour, pale yellow or salmon
H. flaccida (*aurantiaca*) – yellow or peach with a dark yellow throat
H. ochroleuca – pale yellow with a deeper yellow throat

Ixia

The corn lilies are popular, colourful plants with thin tough leaves and wiry stems 25–45 cm (10–18 in) tall carrying short spikes of upright or outward-facing starry flowers in a range of often intense colours. Although they are naturally winter-growers for planting in autumn, corms are

frequently offered by nurserymen for spring planting, in which case they will flower in summer. In mild places they are best planted out in the open ground, but where there are heavy frosts a slightly heated glasshouse or conservatory is necessary, growing them in beds or containers. Few of the wild species are available through nurseries, but some can be obtained from the more specialist firms and societies. Some named hybrids are available, such as: 'Blue Bird' (white with blackish eye, striped violet outside), 'Castor' (purple with yellow eye), 'Hogarth' (white with purple centre), 'Marquette' (yellow with purple centre and tips), 'Rose Emperor' (pink, with darker pink exterior), 'Venus' (magenta with a dark eye).

I. maculata – yellow or orange with brown to black centres
I. rapunculoides – bluish-lavender, flowering early in winter
I. viridiflora – vivid green flowers with a blackish-purple eye

Lachenalia

The exciting Cape cowslips are perhaps more like hyacinths, with fleshy basal leaves that are often prominently blotched, and dense 10–20 cm (4–8 in) spikes of short bell-shaped to long tubular flowers, sometimes pendent, sometimes standing out horizontally and sometimes erect. They are very satisfactory as winter- to spring-flowering pot plants in a cool conservatory, but in mild, frost-free areas can be used for bedding, or even for naturalizing, in the open. Cultivation is very simple in a sandy well-drained soil, but they must be given plenty of light to keep them compact and encourage the intensity of the leaf blotches.

L. aloides – variably coloured pendent bells with blotched leaves
var. *aurea* – golden yellow
var. *quadricolor* – yellow and reddish, tipped maroon and green
'Nelsonii' – yellow, tipped green
'Pearsonii' – orange with reddish-maroon tips
L. bulbifera – pendent tubular bells, red, tipped green; midwinter
L. contaminata – short horizontal bells in white, tipped brown
L. purpureo-caerulea – mid-violet fragrant bells; late spring
L. viridiflora – extraordinary greenish-blue shades

Lapeirousia

Fairly dwarf plants with narrow leaves and much-branched flower stems carrying many small flowers, which have a slender tube and six spreading petals that are usually marked with splashes of contrasting colour (sometimes only three of them). There are many species but few are in cultivation outside specialist collections.

L. oreogena – upright long-tubed flowers, violet with white marks

Massonia

Fascinating, very compact plants with two broad leaves resting on the ground, between which arises in midwinter a stemless 'shaving brush' cluster of flowers

with long-protruding stamens. In some species the leaves are covered with small warts. These are almost hardy and have survived light frosts with me; they are better viewed raised up on a bench in containers. Wide, shallow pans suit them best to allow the leaves to develop properly.

M. depressa – smooth leaves and cream-coloured flowers
M. pustulata – whitish-pink flowers and attractive warty leaves

Melasphaerula

Not one of the most exciting of the Cape bulbs, but graceful and very easy to grow, and flowers over a long period during late winter and early spring. It is 20–30 cm (8–12 in) tall with flat fans of narrow leaves and loosely branched flowering stems.

M. graminea – many small, pendent straw-yellow cone-like bells

Moraea

These might be thought of as the African equivalent of the irises, with gorgeous flowers having three large outer petals and three small inner ones. There are many species in a great array of colours and sizes, flowering over a long period from autumn through winter into spring. Although the individual flowers are fairly short-lived, several are usually produced in succession.

M. aristata – white with dark blue blotch on each outer petal
M. bellendenii – bright yellow, spotted brown in centre
M. loubseri – purple with hairy black patches on outer petals
M. ramosissima – many yellow flowers on tall, branched stems
M. villosa – variable purple-blue with dark 'peacock' markings

Top: There are many lachenalias in a wide range of colours, easily cultivated and flowering in winter and spring. This is *L. bulbifera*.

Bottom: The moraeas are fascinating plants in the Iris family, with a wide range of colours and markings. This is one of the 'peacock moraeas'.

Nerine

The nerines are best known in gardens for the frost-hardy species *N. bowdenii* (see page 102), but there are other attractive species that are hardy outside in mild areas and very suitable for pot cultivation in a frost-free conservatory in colder regions. The species nearly all flower in autumn, with umbels of glistening pink flowers which often have undulate petals. They come in a great range of sizes and there are many hybrids in vivid colours not represented in the wild. For most of them, watering should be reduced after they have died down, although some have more or less evergreen leaves and need a little water from time to time. Feeding with a weak sulphate of potash solution (or potash-rich tomato fertilizer) in the growing season is helpful in encouraging flowers.

N. flexuosa 'Alba' – pure-white crinkly flowers, 20–30 cm (8–12 in)
N. masoniorum – charming miniature, 15–25 cm (6–10 in), with thread-like leaves
N. sarniensis – intense scarlet-red, 30–40 cm (12–16 in)

Ornithogalum

This is a very large genus from Europe, western Asia, tropical Africa and South Africa. There are a few summer-growing species from the eastern Cape region but the majority of them are winter-growers, and most of the Eurasian species are very hardy for growing outdoors. The south-west Cape species are also winter-growers but are not very frost-hardy, so in cold winter areas they are grown mainly under glass. Although the familiar chincherinchee, *O. thyrsoides* – which is seen frequently as a cut flower in florists' shops – is one of these and should therefore be planted in autumn, it has become regular practice for nurserymen in Europe to offer dried bulbs for spring planting, these flowering later on in summer. The bulbs are then lifted and dried over the winter months for replanting once the danger of frost has passed. Alternatively, they can be planted in pots in autumn in a conservatory for spring flowering or, in mild areas, grown outside all year round.

O. dubium – large yellow or orange cupped flowers, 20–35 cm (8–14 in)
O. thyrsoides – conical heads of many white flowers, 25–40 cm (10–16 in)

Polyxena

Small plants, really only suitable for growing in pots on account of their size, although very easy and valuable in that they flower soon after the first watering in autumn following a summer dormancy. They are almost frost-hardy, so require minimal heat in cold areas, just to keep them a degree or so above freezing throughout the winter while they are in leaf. They have short spikes of small funnel-shaped flowers, only 5–8 cm (2–3⅛ in) in height.

P. corymbosa – lilac-pink flowers, striped darker, narrow leaves
P. ensifolia – narrow to broad leaves, white fragrant flowers

Romulea

Compared with the mostly fairly mundane, hardy Northern Hemisphere species (see page 55), many of the Cape romuleas are spectacular plants with large funnel-shaped flowers in a range of brilliant colours. They make ideal container plants for a frost-free conservatory, although they can be grown outside in mild areas, bearing in mind that they need siting in a place where they will receive plenty of sun if the crocus-like flowers are to open out properly. In the low light intensity of British winters I find that they sometimes barely open at all. A sandy potting soil seems to suit most, dried out thoroughly during the summer.

R. atrandra – large, yellow-eyed, pinkish-magenta flowers
R. sabulosa – bright red with a black centre, marked yellow
R. saldanhensis – bright, shiny yellow

Sparaxis

These, the harlequin flowers, are winter-growers, flowering in spring and therefore normally planted in autumn, but the corms can often be found on sale in spring for summer flowering. This may work for the first season, but they try to change back to their normal season if left in the ground. They are nearly frost-hardy so, even in cold areas, it is worth trying some of the vigorous hybrids outside in a sheltered sunny position. Otherwise, they make excellent, showy plants for a cool conservatory. They have fans of narrow

The very dwarf, easily cultivated *Polyxena corymbosa* flowers in the autumn or early winter and is one of the first of all the Cape bulbs to flower.

sword-shaped leaves and short spikes of large (5–6 cm/2–2½ in diameter), flattish, brightly coloured flowers, mostly on 20–30 cm (8–12 in) stems.

S. elegans – salmon-orange with a blackish eye and yellow zone
S. grandiflora – very variable, a wide range of brilliant colours
S. tricolor – orange or pinkish with darker and yellow zones

Strumaria

See *Hessea* on page 120.

Tritonia

Like *Sparaxis*, these are naturally winter-growers, but in Europe nurserymen sometimes sell dried corms for planting in spring after the frosts have finished. If planted in autumn, in cold areas, they are best treated as container plants for an attractive display in late winter or spring; but in mild areas they can simply be planted in the open, since the more commonly available ones are very easily cultivated in ordinary, well-drained soil. They grow 20–40 cm (8–16 in) in height with short spikes of wide, saucer-shaped flowers and upright fans of narrow sword-like leaves.

T. crocata – orange or salmon-orange
T. lineata – creamy-yellow or near-white with grey veining
T. squalida – pale pink with a darker throat

Veltheimia

These striking plants are excellent for containers in a slightly heated conservatory, although they will grow outside in areas that are frost-free. They are winter-growers, making their new leaf growth and flowering in late autumn, winter or spring, then going into a summer rest period. The leaves of *V. capensis* disappear completely for the summer and it should be dried out during this period, but *V. bracteata* is more or less evergreen and requires a little water throughout the summer as well. The large bulbs are planted in early autumn with their tips just out of the soil, or half-exposed in the case of *V. capensis*, in a well-drained loam-based medium. They have basal tufts of leaves and dense 30–40 cm (12–16 in) spikes of tubular flowers, rather like those of the red-hot poker.

V. bracteata – bright shiny green leaves, pinkish-red flowers
V. capensis – narrower, wavy grey leaves, pink flowers
V. 'Lemon Flame' – pale yellow flowers
V. 'Rosalba' – creamy-yellow flowers, suffused pink near the base

Gloriosa superba **is, indeed, a superb plant for the conservatory but requires a trellis or sticks on which to climb by means of tendrils.**

TENDER AND TROPICAL:
AN INTRODUCTION TO BULBS FOR THE CONSERVATORY

The extent to which the more tender bulbs require protection depends very much on where the garden is situated, so it is impossible to lay down hard-and-fast rules about what will grow where. In frosty-winter parts of Europe and North America it will be necessary to grow all but the very toughest of bulbs under heated glass, whereas in the Mediterranean region, in the southern and south-western United States, in much of Australia and in North Island, New Zealand, a lot of the bulbs regarded as tender elsewhere can be grown outside. As with practically every aspect of gardening, it is a case of trying things out in your own locality, and how enjoyable it is to try and prove the books and the pundits quite wrong!

The bulbs that I am describing below may therefore well be plants for a heated conservatory in some places, but there will be many gardeners who can grow them outside and for whom a conservatory may be just too hot in summer to grow anything at all.

Cyrtanthus elatus, often known as Vallota, is a very successful pot plant for the conservatory but in mild countries can be grown outside in the dappled shade.

Bulbs from the more tropical regions of the world differ markedly in their behaviour from those from temperate climates, in that they do not have a built-in reaction to cold and warm seasons, only to wet or dry ones. This means that they can be induced into growth at almost any time of the year by keeping them warm and dry, and then watering them again. For those gardening in temperate areas, this is quite useful since, if required, the bulbs can be kept in a warm place throughout the cold winter months and then brought out and grown for the summer, thus dispensing with the need for expensive heating in a conservatory during the winter.

TENDER AND TROPICAL BULBS

Brunsvigia

These could have been incorporated into the chapter on Cape bulbs, since they are South African and are mainly winter-growers, producing large umbels on 20 cm (8 in) stems of pink or red funnel-shaped flowers in late summer or early autumn before the broad leaves appear. In mild-winter areas they can be grown outside, but in colder climates they need protection and make interesting subjects for a frost-free conservatory, planted in large, deep containers of well-drained sandy soil. In order to flower well they need a warm dry period in summer while they are leafless. After flowering they are grown through the winter at a minimum of about 8°C (47°F).

B. josephinae – rosy-red, funnel-shaped flowers in large umbels
B. minor – bright pink

Chlidanthus

This may be hardy in really mild gardens, but container cultivation in a heated glasshouse or conservatory is necessary in colder areas. It needs a sunny well-drained situation or, if in containers, a loam-based sandy potting medium with regular liquid feeds of a potash-rich fertilizer when in growth. The bulbs are planted in spring after a winter dormancy and come into growth soon after. They produce strap-like greyish leaves and few-flowered umbels on stems up to 30 cm (12 in). They come from South America.

C. fragrans – fragrant, yellow funnel-shaped flowers

to have their large colourful
winter, so many bulbs are sc
nurserymen in the autumn
in winter. Most of those ma
hybrids, in an array of colou
and creamy-yellow to pink a
sometimes strongly striped
background. Some of the sp
cultivated, but mainly by sp
enthusiasts. The large bulbs
a light, open potting mediu
the bulb exposed; liquid fee
rich fertilizer are beneficial i
flower bud formation. Som
related genus, *Rhodophiala*,
cultivated. These are similar
generally smaller flowers an
one or two of them hardy e
a small amount of frost, but
very little cultivated. Hippe
mostly from tropical South
whereas the rhodophialas cc
more temperate areas of the

H. papilio – 45–50 cm (18–
with white flowers, stained
maroon
H. reginae – 45–60 cm (18
two to four slightly droopir
H. reticulatum – 30 cm (12
six reddish-purple net-veine
H. rutilum – 30 cm (12 in),
four crimson-red or orange
H. 'Apple Blossom' – very l
petal with a paler band
H. 'Picotee' – white with re
to the petals
H. 'Star of Holland' – large
a white central star
H. 'White Dazzler' – pure v

Crinum

A large group of mainly tropical and
subtropical bulbs of very exotic appearance,
with umbels of large, often showy, fragrant
long-tubed, funnel-shaped flowers. Most
of those in cultivation are large plants with
bold foliage and stout leafless stems up to
1 m (3¼ ft) or more in height, so if grown
in a conservatory these are plants for large
containers. The long-necked, sometimes
enormous, bulbs are planted with the
necks protruding from the soil. The species
most commonly encountered, *C. moorei*,
C. bulbispermum and their hybrid
C. × powellii, will take light frosts and
will be found in the summer section on
page 80, but they also make good container
plants for the cool conservatory or patio.
These three crinums are summer-growers
and require plenty of moisture at this time
of year, with a rest in winter, although in
the case of *C. moorei* and *C. × powellii* a
little water should be given at all times,
since they are more or less evergreen, dying
back a little but not completely, unless
frosted. In containers, regular liquid feeds
with a tomato-type (high potash) fertilizer
are beneficial in maintaining vigour.
The more tropical species, such as
C. asiaticum and its relatives, can be grown
in large containers but require lots of
moisture, frequent feeding (every two
weeks with a balanced N:P:K – nitrogen,
phosphate and potash) and much higher
temperatures – 15°C (59°F) minimum
in winter. Crinums are widespread in the
tropics and subtropics.

C. asiaticum – up to 1.5 m (5 ft) tall, with
umbels of starry white flowers
C. bulbispermum – up to fifteen drooping
white, pink-striped flowers
C. moorei – wide-open white or pinkish
flowers 15–20 cm (6–8 in) across
C. × powellii – rich pink, funnel-shaped
fragrant flowers
C. × powellii 'Album' – the lovely pure-
white version

Cyrtanthus

These attractive members of the amaryllis
family are not widely cultivated as
yet, although they have considerable
ornamental value, and the hybrids that
are appearing are likely to increase their
popularity. Most of them have strap-like
leaves and 20–30 cm (8–12 in) stems
carrying few-flowered umbels of colourful
tubular to funnel-shaped flowers, generally
3–5 cm (1¼–2 in) long. The most widely
cultivated species is *C. elatus*, the George
lily, Knysna lily or Scarborough lily, which
is more familiar under the name *Vallota
speciosa*. This is a superb pot plant for
a heated conservatory, although it does
not require a great amount of warmth in
winter, since its growing and flowering
periods are in spring and summer. During
the winter it has a partial rest period, but
it is evergreen so a little water is required at
intervals; a minimum temperature of about
10°C (50°F) is sufficient. It is best to leave
the bulbs to increase over a period of
several years to fill the pots, giving them
liquid high-potash (tomato-type) feeds in
summer. In regions with frost-free winters
C. elatus can be tried outside in sheltered,

dappled shade. *Cyrtanthus* are from
southern Africa and tropical East Africa.

C. elatus – up to five funnel-shaped scarlet
flowers, 6–9 cm (2½–3½ in) across
C. elatus 'Delicata' – a soft pink version

Eucharis

Lovely summer- to autumn-flowering
tropical bulbs with bold, glossy green oval
leaves and stout stems up to 60 cm (2 ft)
high, carrying several fragrant white flowers
up to 10 cm (4 in) across, with six petals
surrounding a cup in the centre. In cool
areas it will be necessary to grow them in
a heated glasshouse (minimum winter
temperature 10°C/50°F) throughout the
year but, if in containers, they can be
placed outside for the summer. They
come from South America.

E. amazonica – the Amazon lily, large
white flowers, 8–10 cm (3⅛–4 in) across

Eucrosia

These tropical members of the amaryllis
family are seldom cultivated, although one
species has become more readily available
in recent years. They have umbels of
brightly coloured tubular or funnel-shaped
flowers with long-protruding stamens,
produced before the broad oval leaves
appear. They are best treated as container
plants for a heated conservatory, given
a dry, warm dormant period (at least
15°C/59°F) in winter, then started into
growth in spring for the summer growing
period. The dormant bulbs are usually

offered in the spring cata
well-drained potting mec
Eucrosia is from Ecuador

E. bicolor – 30–40 cm (1
with umbels of reddish-c

Gloriosa

Known as the flame lily,
colour and shape of its p
climbing plant is of the
either outside in very wa
container plant in a hea
(minimum 10°C/50°F).
tubers are usually obtair
planting following their
and are planted in a wel
position where they will
moisture in their summ
It will need some adjace
which to climb or, if in
twigs or a trellis. In win
be withheld and the tul
The slender leafy stems
(6½–9¾ ft) in height wi
pendent red, orange or
which the petals are sha
wavy at the edges. It is
and India.

**Above: The
hippeastrums, which
are often sold as
'Amaryllis', are mostly
from tropical South
America so require
warm growing
conditions and a
warm, dry dormancy.
Shown here is H.
papilio from Brazil.**